WABI-SABI

A BEGINNER'S GUIDE TO THE ART OF SIMPLICITY AND TAKING PLEASURE IN SIMPLE THINGS

without contract or any type of guarantee assurance.

The trademarks that are used are without any consent, and the publication of the trademark is without permission or backing by the trademark owner. All trademarks and brands within this book are for clarifying purposes only and are the owned by the owners themselves, not affiliated with this document.

Contents

INTRODUCTION

Wabi-sabi is like a sweet old Zen tale, in many ways. It's an articulation of the beauty that lies in the brief transition between life's ups and downs, both the joy and the melancholy that make up our lot as humans.

Wabi-sabi is a stylistic concept and theory that is best understood in terms of the Zen tradition that, over the last thousand years, has nurtured and shaped its creation. Zen attempts artistic expression in ways as pure and sacred as the Zen teachings they manifest; it rejects intellectualism yet pretense and instead strives to uncover and picture the simplicity created by nature's flows.

Wabi-sabi represents the cosmic Zen nihilist view and seeks beauty in the flaws found as all things evolve from nothing in a constant state of flux, and return to nothingness. Within this never-ending movement, nature leaves for us to contemplate arbitrary tracks, and it is these random flaws and irregularities that offer a model for the modest and humble expression of elegance in wabi-sabi. Wabi-sabi's practice, firmly rooted in Zen philosophy, utilizes the evanescence of life to express the feeling of haunting beauty provided by such an interpretation.

The Zen monks combined the worlds of art and philosophy as early as the thirteenth century into a symbiotic whole where the two functions and goals became almost indivisible. Since then, Japanese culture has been an unstoppable creative force rivaling any other country's influence on world culture and art. For a nation one-thirtieth the size of the United States, the scope of its distinctions–in almost any field of the arts–is quite astounding.

The impact of Wabi-sabi on Japanese aesthetic values has influenced such arts as the tea ceremony, flower arrangement, haiku, landscape design, and No theatre. This provides an artistic vision that utilizes the intransigent hand of death to focus the mind on the sublime fleeting perfection that is impermanent in all matters. It can be found in the arrangement of a single flower, the expression of deep emotion in three lines of literature, or the perception of a single rock mountain landscape. The same as Zen, her mentor in philosophy, Wabi-sabi is phenomenal in its subtlety.

The term wabi-sabi indicates impermanence, humility, asymmetry, and imperfection. Such underlying principles are diametrically opposed to those of their Western counterparts, whose beliefs are grounded in a Hellenic ethos that emphasizes longevity, grandeur, harmony and beauty.

Infused with the philosophy of wabi-sabi, Japanese sculpture finds meaning in the realities of the natural world, searching for its motivation against nature.

To discover the unadorned truth of nature, it refrains from all forms of intellectual entanglement, self-consciousness, and affectation. Since by its asymmetry and random imperfections existence can be identified, wabi-sabi seeks the beauty of natural imperfection.

The Japanese development of this philosophy to art has produced an artistic expression resonating with a deep philosophical continuity— a consistency of great historical complexity little influenced by evolving trends and styles. From woodblock prints that influenced contemporary artists such as Monet and Van Gogh to the culinary arts that paved the way for modern cooking, from the many styles of martial arts to Kurosawa's cinematic epic Seven Samurai, from the haiku poetry that motivated Gary Snyder to the world-fascinating landscape fashion, Japan's influence on the West has been prolific— and it has been bright.

Despite the ever-invasive materiality of Western society, the concept of wabi-sabi is as relevant today as it was in Japan in the thirteenth century. This classical approach to life, which breathes new definition into both the artistic and decorative arts, is indifferent to modern Western culture, choosing a more straightforward theory and nature ethic for our shortcomings and organic existence instead.

The continuity between the concepts of theory and design ensures that the concept of wabi-sabi is still important for many elements of modern culture.

Wabi-sabi is a core element of Japanese people's aesthetic sense and gentle nature. It's a belief system that guides the way they live life, though it's rarely talked about. The presence is everywhere and yet it can be seen nowhere. People intuitively know what the wabi-sabi concept stands for, but few can express that. Wabi-sabi is a mysterious enigma that aims to whisper important insight to those who are patient enough to explore and view it with an open mind.

Society has gathered pace in recent years, our levels of stress have gone through the roof, and we have become increasingly obsessed with money, job titles, appearances and the endless accumulation of things. There's an increasing sense of dissatisfaction as we press ourselves harder and synchronize more. They are overstretched, overworked and exhausted.

As somebody who has spent the past couple of years helping people reorient their goals and build a life based on doing what they enjoy, I've witnessed how many of us grow sick of over-commitment, constant reference, criticism and anxiety and self-talk. We stumble through our days, eyes dulled, and much of our time co-oping in bins, paying more attention to actors, ads and social media than discovering our own lives, in all their rich capacity.

I have heard the rising rumblings of a progressive transition for some time now, a yearning for a simpler, more fulfilling life. That existence filled with grace, linked with nature, reverberating with the vitality of daily health and centered on what truly counts for us. The more tired, frustrated and dissatisfied people that came to me, the more I felt the need for a new approach to problems, and open resources that would help us lead more honest and motivated lives.

It told me of the inherent elegance, calmness and gratitude I haven't experienced anywhere else in Japan, indicating life lessons hidden in the traditional kimono's sleeves. I suspected that the elusive concept of wabi-sabi might have something to do with it, so I set out to discover the deep truth.

As I said it is a tricky endeavor to try to articulate a definition of wabi-sabi. It's a bit like love–I can tell you what I think it's and how it feels to me, but you really know only when you feel it for yourself.

Nearly without exception, conversations I had with Japanese people about this subject started with:' Wabi-sabi? Hmmm... It's very hard to explain.' And the truth is, most people have never tried to articulate it, and they don't see the need to. They grew up with it. It's the way they perceive the world and enjoy the magic. It's integrated into who they really are.

None to deflate from a challenge, though, I pushed on. Well, I was actually waiting, I was watching and I was listening. The more room I gave people to explore the significance of this unspoken thing that was so familiar to them, the more it became interesting. Metaphors, hand gestures and head tilting. Hands on hearts and long pauses, as well as repeated references to tea and Zen and essence. The discussion often came to an end with:' I would like to read your book.' Needless to say, there is no universal definition of wabi-sabi in Japanese. Any effort to convey that will only ever be from the person's perspective who describes it.

My own experience is that of someone who is both a Japanologist and a therapist in the unusual position. Throughout my effort to distill the wabi-sabi concepts into a collection of open life lessons, I spoke with people from all walks of existence, pored through books throughout ancient libraries, toured museums, meditated in dark temples, kept tea cups in my lap, spent time in nature and walked around Japanese architecture centuries-old. I have developed a series of guiding principles through hundreds of discussions and extensive research that I believe will be valuable lessons for all of us. Inside this book you can find them all.

Wabi-sabi originated in the 15th century, and began as a reaction to the lavishness, ornamentation, and rich materials that constituted the predominant ethos at the period. Wabi-sabi is hard to decipher, but has been described as "the most prominent and characteristic aspect of traditional Japanese beauty and occupies roughly the same place in the Japanese pantheon of esthetic principles as do the Greek ideals of beauty and elegance in the West," by Leonard Koren, who wrote one of the first books to bring wabi-sabi to the United states. The expression is a mixture of the terms "wabi" and "sabi," all of which have their own senses complicated to interpret. Wabi implies purity, modesty and living in harmony with nature. It can be used to describe someone who is satisfied with little and is making the most of what they have. Sabi makes reference to what happens over time. It's about transience and the age-old beauty and authenticity. Practicing sabi means learning to accept the natural cycle of growth, death, and the imperfections that accompany that development. Together the two terms create a feeling in the uncomplicated, unassuming, mysterious and ephemeral that finds harmony and serenity.

For a long time the Japanese had learned the tricks to leading an easy, authentic life. One need only look at their typical tea ceremonies ' meticulous attention and respect to see a wonderful example that fully celebrates the practice of slowness. It was the simple act of making a cup of tea which brought to life the centuries-old Japanese wabi-sabi philosophy, whose roots lie in Zen Buddhism and Taoism.

Fighting back against the ancient chinese tea ceremonies which embodied an elite, ostentatious opulence, Japanese tea master of the 16th century and Zen monk Murata Shuko began conducting ceremonies which were exactly the opposite. Using rustic, coarse and unrefined tools set in sparse, basic furnishings, he emphasized the notion of simplicity and was present in the process itself: to fetch water, to collect wood for the fire, to boil water, to make tea and to serve to others. Many Japanese tea masters and Zen monks started to teach likewise, and gradually the implicit teachings in the revamped tea ceremony became a doctrine itself, widely known as wabi-sabi.

The real meaning of "wabi" is rather vague, but it has often been used to characterize someone who was satisfied with having very little in existence, and who was stripped of ambition, rage and addiction to material object. "Sabi" refers to the impermanence of time and the acceptance of the cycle of growth, decay, and death — objects that have aged with a certain grace and dignity, bearing the brunt of time with elegance.

Wabi-sabi is not sleek and made in mass production. It is about seeing the elegance in the bad, and encouraging nature's asymmetry and perishable natural materials. As such, wabi-sabi design features entail ruggedness, ease, efficiency, discipline, and humility. The often cited example of wabi-sabi's manifestation is Hagi ware— the Japanese pottery used in many tea ceremonies. The pieces are often rustic and simple-looking with not quite symmetrical shapes, and colors or textures that seem to underline an unrefined or simple style. History is a big part of wabi-sabi, so buying new, hand distressed products doesn't fit the bill. The wear has to come with true age and time influence. The presence of cracks and scratches in things is considered and is to be embraced as symbolic of the passing of time, weather and loving usage.

Although wabi-sabi is perhaps too embedded with a traditional ideology to be called a phenomenon itself, we can definitely see wabi-sabi's aesthetics growing in popularity. From the outside it looks like the clean, uncluttered minimalist spaces but with a little bit more of a welcoming personality. The key to true wabi-sabi is genuineness. You really have to embrace the rough edges and imperfections that time leaves on your objects if you want to embody the wabi-sabi style in your home. So if you love transience and antique items that actually show their era, or just want to be more in harmony with nature, then give wabi-sabi an attempt.

We consider the tech world to be rational, run by rules of business and technical realities. We think that people are more or less predictable: inspired by certain obvious factors-challenging work, a pleasant climate, positive feedback.

The error we make is that, especially at work, we can never know someone in whole. People are biological, mental, guided by deep forces which do not emerge in the professional world until the cracks are too big to hide.

Wabi-Sabi is an acknowledgement of the defects which form an integral part of nature.

The ideals apply to design, too. We should find their wear and tear as a symbol of something well liked before we throw away the jumper with the void in the collar, or those torn jeans. Instead of getting rid of them, mend them and take pride in their patches, frayed edges, missing buttons and faded fabric. Buy things as investments rather than as part of disposable, fleeting trends, and–most importantly–appreciate where things are made and how.

Yet wabi-sabi isn't just confined to the tangible, the actual. So often in response to someone's weakness or failure we utter the phrase "Well, nobody's perfect" as a defense. But why shouldn't something be said in celebration? After all, what makes us human is a willingness to learn from our mistakes, and to rise when we're down. We are flawed and that is really where our beauty lies.

Wabi-sabi can be seen anywhere, just like elegance, if we only take the time to adjust our outlook. And above all, move effortlessly on the world, live steadily and easily, and in this moment rejoice wholeheartedly — for it will also pass.

More than anything else in this manuscript, wabi-sabi has been the easiest to pin down and interpret as a philosophy, a style and a way of life.

The original meaning of wabi refers to the feeling of remote isolation which comes with living in nature, and the paradoxical beauty of imperfection (like a broken cup fixed with gold, by kintsugi).

Depending on the context, Sabi may mean "withered," "light" or "cooled," but more often applies to the elegance of ageing–such as the shifting color of oak, the comeliness of stone, the delicate droop and the drying of roses in the heat. For me, Wabi-sabi is like being inside when it rains outside; the lines of amusement on a face; or after a quick meal, feeling happily sated.

It's much easier to express the meaning of what wabi-sabi is as opposed to what it isn't.

CHAPTER ONE: THE BEGINNING, HISTORY OF WABI-SABI

In ancient China, the Taoists tried to make the most of their lives by living in harmony with nature in a very practical and Chinese way. It was only by studying the natural flows of life that they could become one with the Tao, the mystical force which guides the lives of all men.

The Tao never stays still like a river. This idea became a basic principle in the universal vision of the Taoists and was to become a trademark not only of the Taoism but of the Zen which followed it. Such deference for the spontaneous and erratic was to find its expression in many fields of artistic endeavors as the art of the day, as it is now, was motivated by the artists ' fundamental religious beliefs. As a product of the Zen mind, Wabi-sabi can find its earliest roots in Zen's forerunner, Taoism, and in these pages we will explore its development from its first impressions in China to the cultural icon it had become in Japan.

Even though the history of wabi-sabi-style art is patchy and difficult to identify, it is possible to pinpoint the Song dynasty (960–1279) as the time when art began to show certain leanings towards the principles of wabi-sabi, even though they may not have been articulated in such words. It was at this point that the first painting of wen-jen hua, or literati, emerged. The literati were novices who, at the Royal Academy, frequently disagreed with the popular trends and created their own distinct scenes. Wen-jen hua's Northern Song practitioners chose fewer grandiose topics than the official painters did, frequently choosing either a single tree or a bamboo and rock. This desire for straightforward subjects was still a characteristic of literati art. The work's brevity and simplicity provided ample room for the audience's mental collaboration and this was to become a defining characteristic of later wabi-sabi creations.

During the dynasty period known as the Southern Song (1127–1279) the painting academy of the emperors produced a landscape style known as the Ma-Hsia College, derived from the two best artists of the time, Ma Yüan and Hsia Kuei. Drawing upon the expansiveness seen in the style of Northern Song, they produced images with much less brushwork. They used mist as an instrument, for example, to suggest landmass and to give the painting a light, ethereal quality. Ma Yüan was often referred to as "one-corner Ma" because he would confine much of his artwork to a single corner of the canvas, leaving the rest void. This technique increased the sensation of open space and suggested infinity, a quality that is highly prized in the tradition of Ma-Hsia.

The Japanese somehow became masters of space, and stressed the importance of nothing or nothingness as a juxtaposition of issues that currently exist in their lengthy cultural past.

As the quietness between notes in music is essential, the space provided in art is just as expressive, and wabi-sabi used brevity to amplify the expression's intensity.

The brush painting of the Ch'an monks stands in sharp contrast to the serenity of Ma Yüan and Hsia Kuei's work (Ch'an is the Chi nese counterpart to Zen, which takes its name from the Sanskrit word for contemplation, dhyana, like Zen). Disciples of this group of Buddhist religion believed in creative improvisation, sometimes making works in frenzied minutes. Official academy painters ridiculed the form, distinguished by free and often loosely defined brushwork, as the work of "mad drunkards." In later centuries, when more artists were disillusioned with the purely academic models, the individuality of the Zen painting school became a significant example. Zen monks also varied drastically from the mainstream because of their deeply different worldviews. This transition away from popular norms was manifested in a key aspect of wabi-sabi design: that of a love for the untraditional — not just because it is unorthodox, but because unconventional art stimulates different ways of interpreting art.

Throughout China, the Zen temples led the way for the arts in Buddhism. A current resident abbot of the Daitokuji temple in Kyoto indicated that one of the first serious steps toward an understanding of physical objects with a modest and rustic charm came at a time when Buddhist monks, whose temples were often under-funded, had to entertain guests. As they did not own any high-quality art, they had to use what was accessible to them to achieve an aesthetically pleasing effect, and to this end nature items such as bamboo and wildflowers were used instead of more ornate pieces such as chinese porcelain.

In doing so, they concentrated on the real, the impermanent, and the modest, and they explored the inherent beauty contained in these plain and often rustic artifacts in the beautiful random patterns produced by nature's movement. The tiny nuances of colour, the curve of an opening petal, the crack in a bamboo vase, or the decay of a knot in old timber all came to symbolize mujo, which is the Buddhist principle of impermanence and continuous flux. These simple objects then became vehicles for aesthetic contemplation, as the physical manifestations of mujo. Wabi-sabi has become the term associated with this quality, forming a defining aspect of wabi-sabi objects as such. If an object or expression can bring about a sense of serene melancholy and a spiritual longing within us, then it could be said that object is wabi-sabi. The Zen monks then sought to understand this by creating artifacts and experiences that used certain attributes to improve one's state of mind.

Architecture and aesthetic ideals came from the Zen monasteries which were then absorbed into the Japanese way of life, and from this era the profusion of arts was more often than not inspired by a Zen master's work. One such art is the tea ceremony, which became a cornerstone of high culture and the expression of beauty in sobriety due to its links with the Zen monk Ikkyu and his school of thought. The craft of ikebana, flower arranging, and raku ceramics originated with the tea ceremony revolution. There have been several flower arrangement schools but the one that best represents the tea ceremony's wabi-sabi feelings is named nagaire (literally to put in). In this college, the arranger follows concepts laid out in other, more regimented schools and instead encourages the nature of the flowers to represent the elegance and evanescence of existence in accordance with the visual characteristics of the vase. Raku-style pottery was introduced into the tea ceremony as a response to the nobility's favored ornate Chinese utensils and stressed the elegance of rustic imperfection over efforts at excellence. It was during this time that Japan's artistry moved into a new age with the popularity of wabi-sabi items hitting their zenith, under the leadership of the tea masters.

There was a more negative influence behind the development of wabi-sabi art in this time as well. The prestige that Kyoto once accumulated as Japan's capital was greatly diminished by the capital's relocation to Kamakura, which is beyond modern Tokyo. Iemoto was the word used by the creators or inheritors of the arts-related scriptures, codes, and cherished scrolls such as music, dance, No theatre, and tea ceremony, and it was through this means that the teachings were handed down through the family. Such privilege also grants the iemoto the right to formal judgment on any legal or scientific level, and as such it was also a lucrative source of income — not entirely different from conventional patents. The sometimes competitive harboring of these artifacts and their prestige has profoundly influenced the way arts evolved in Japan. On the one hand, it has retained a degree of consistency from the original teachings and in some instances upheld the original orthodox practices; on the other hand, it has at times been corrupted by political and financial interests, and then strays away from the original meaning conceived by the founding father. Strict obedience to Sen no Rikyu's ideas (see later discussion of the tea ceremony) has contributed to certain elements of the tea ceremony being devoid of any real spiritual union— the fundamental explanation for its existence.

This has also been proposed that some of the mystery and intrigue around the etheric properties of wabi-sabi art was deliberately cultivated by the iemoto families whose profits had been severely diminished by Kamakura's emergence. Without the funds for the more ornate and magnificent artifacts, the iemoto families turned their attention to the wabi-sabi-style art that was readily available, and then enhanced its value by enveloping it in riddle. Therefore, the iemoto family's efforts played a significant role in promoting wabi-sabi as an art for the refined. And wabi-sabi has become an art form that offered far greater potential for those who were willing to uncover beauty in what might at first glance have been considered unsophisticated and unattractive.

The gears were now set in motion from this golden era of painting for the transition of beauty ideals to all facets of Japanese culture. The key philosophy of finding beauty in detail was now incorporated into the Japanese mind, where it remained relatively unchallenged until Japan opened its borders to the West once again.

The Japanese, the consummate artists of observation, learned very quickly from the West and Japan established itself as a force to be reckoned with within a few decades. Although she assimilated Western wisdom, Japan was able to pass new ideas through the prism of its own society and then take the best that was given to each. This phenomenon has been going on down through the ages, and one of the biggest talents in Japan today is to take an international innovation, adapt it, and then market it back to the West.

The changes brought to Japan by the West were disruptive and changed almost beyond comprehension styles of dress and practices. Japan was prepared to sacrifice much of its culture in her desire to catch up with and participate more fully in the Western hedonism.

There was also a narrowly defeated vote at one point as to whether the Japanese should maintain their own language or switch to English. Fortunately, the language has been retained, and it has continued to function as a bridge between past and present. Without it, there would surely have been a lot of Japanese culture lost. The people of Japan have managed to retain a small nugget of Japanese-ness knitted into the fabric of their words and deeds with the help of the language and a great personal pride in their cultural heritage. They may have been greatly affected by the West, yet they are still predominantly Japanese, and this can be seen in the different ways in which they still view research and architecture.

Even in modern designs today the Japanese attention to detail and their desire to keep all aspects of design as simple and well balanced as possible are evident. The cultural norms that bound the Japanese through their remarkable history remain ingrained in the national psyche and the way they see themselves, and their Zen roots still strongly influence the objects they design and make.

In Japanese, there is an expression that says that someone who makes things of poor quality is actually worse than a thief, because he doesn't make things that will last or bring true satisfaction. At least a thief redistributes the richness of a society.

The connection between modern-day designs and the ancient wabi-sabi designs may seem a little tenuous, but there is a slightly changed perception of values in the spirit with which both are approached and the reverence given for the creativity process.

And it is these principles that have provided Japan with an excellent base for its relationship with the modern world that have their origins in the Zen so wabi-sabi concepts.

CHAPTER TWO: THE INDOCTRINATION OF THE ZEN AND BUDDHISM IN WABI-SABI

Because Zen has been the guiding light for Japanese meditation and theory for over a thousand years, it has also established the spiritual and esthetic foundation for all Japanese practices since they progressed over the centuries. It has become embedded in the Japanese aesthetic sensibility through its impact on the aristocracy and the leading creative figures throughout the decades. So a detailed look at Zen and its creation in Japan will shed some further light on wabi-sabi's artistic philosophy.

Based in northeastern India, Buddhism was based on the teachings of Siddhartha Gautama, now regarded as the Buddha, or the Enlightened Being.

Birthed into a luxury life in 563 b.c. He was so moved by the pain of those outside the palace that he was motivated to give up the material world to seek answers to the life's mysteries. Upon going through a period of intense asceticism, the Buddha took the middle route, which resisted both the traps of overindulgence and personality-denial, and is said to have attained enlightenment under a bodhi tree after a great struggle.

Knowing the nature of reality, he started teaching and developing an ideology based on the Four Noble Truths, including the Four Noble Truths 1. Life's going to hurt.

2. All misery is caused by ignorance of the nature of reality and the ensuing want, addiction, and grip that derives from this ignorance.

3. Overcoming indifference and one's addiction to the material world will stop suffering.

4. The path leading away from pain is the Noble Eightfold Path, which comprises of right views, right thought, right expression, right action, right life, right commitment, right mindset and right meditation.

Throughout the years, these concepts were transmitted through one practitioner to another, but Zen Buddhism was to be influenced by China, where the Buddhist theories were to experience radical changes when they went through a society that already had powerful religious and cultural ideas on its own.

The Chinese Taoist movement merged with new ideas emerging from India to create the Buddhist Ch'an school, and this later became established in Japan as Zen. The basic metaphysical and spiritual principles of the Taoist are to be found in the Tao-te Ching (Classic of the Way and Its Power), a document dated about the third century B.C.

Yet referred to the historical figure of Lao-tzu, as well as to the Chuang-tzu, published in the same period yet assigned to the author Chuang-tzu.

Taoism was characterized as "the art of being in the universe," and its teaching's main thrust was opposed to the Confucian views on social structure. Rather, it emphasized that the person would try to flow along with the way of the watercourse, known as the Tao. Lao-tzu defined this spiritual definition in the following way, which like Zen defies objective analysis: The Tao is something elusive and indefinable How unquantifiable! How unclear it is!

But, there is a structure in it.

So obscure, so indefinable But there is something in it.

So quiet! Too comprehensive!

Yet there is a material in it.

The material is real, The honesty in it.

The term never departs from the old until now, Whereby it inspects all items.

How in their essence do I learn these things?

It is for this purpose.

—Daisetz Suzuki, for Zen and Japanese Culture

To be in harmony with the Tao, one must follow wu-wei and keep from causing anything to happen that doesn't happen by itself.

To be at one with the Tao is to agree that we have to give in to a force much greater than we are. By embracing the natural flow of life, and discarding all learned doctrines and wisdom, an individual may attain true harmony with the Tao. That equilibrium carries with it a mystical power known as To-, which enables those who have harnessed it to look beyond the horizons of daily experience into a realm where there is no simplistic difference between all of the dualistic world's opposing ideas.

The Taoists tried to extend their lives through alchemy, physical practices, strict grooming, and breathing exercises during the period before the introduction of Buddhist concepts from the Indian subcontinent, but under the influence of Buddhism, Taoist religious groups moved more towards formal monasticism. There's also a change from the emphasis on physical immortality to the Buddhists promising divine immortality.

It is believed that the convergence of Taoism with Buddhist concepts was influenced by the advent of the unconventional monk identified as the Bodhi-dharma (referred to as the Daruma throughout Japan). Bodhidharma was twenty-eighth in the straight line from the first Buddhist follower, Kas-yapa, and when he took his Buddhist form to China in 527, it was to launch ripples that sent shock waves not only to China, but also to Japan across the oceans.

After arriving in China, Bodhidharma was given an audience with Emperor Wu, who clearly was requesting the Indian monk's appreciation for the devotional work he thought he had accomplished. But much to the surprise of the expectant emperor, the sage, when asked if there was any value in constructing temples and copying scriptures, responded, "No benefit." Deflated by the sudden and unwelcome reaction, the emperor then asked Bodhidharma who was this man standing before him, to whom Bodhidharma answered, "I don't know, Your Majesty." Myth has it that he was so determined to succeed in his awakening that when they prevented him from staying awake whilst meditating he sliced off his own eyelids. It is also part of legend that he has been meditating for so long that his arms and legs fall off, and that is why red papier-mâché models without hands or arms is used to represent the Daruma in Japan.

A man called Shang Kwang, who was following Bodhidharma's knowledge, demanded that he may be allowed to research under him. While he stayed for a week in the freezing air, it wasn't until he cut off his own left arm and displayed it as a sign of his willingness to know that Bodhidharma relented and passed on his experience to the person who was about to become his successor.

The realistic and focused Chinese thinkers of that time tried to demystify Indian Buddhism's rather ethereal teachings and to create a framework that would allow the great insights to be harnessed in a more practical way. The gathering of the three religions of Buddhism, Confucianism, and Taoism was portrayed in the famous image of the vinegar tasters where Sakyamuni (the name given to the Buddha), Confucius, and Lao-tzu stood around a big vinegar vat which symbolized life. Confucius considered it sour, the Buddha thought it bitter but it was called sweet by the Taoist Lao-tzu. Taoism means trying to accept things as they are, to see beauty and wonder in the midst of the earthly.

While Zen is a Buddhist philosophy in origin, Taoism's influence has been immense and far-reaching, and the two philosophies are similar in essence than Zen and other Buddhist philosophies. Many shun formality and schooling, and both promote a return to the natural state of non-dualismby transcending our common view of the world to see truth as it is.

As early as 538, the first seeds of Buddhism were sown in Japan when the King of Korea sent a delegation to Japan that included some Buddhist sutras. It was the Soga family of Japan who actively sought to promote the doctrines, but their attempts were impeded by the influential Mononobe family, who believed that the adoption of a foreign religion would threaten the local gods. The spread of Buddhism began in earnest when the Soga family gained military and political supremacy over the Mononobe family in the ensuing century.

It was Prince Shotoku, Emperor Yomei's second son, whose role in establishing monasteries made his name associated with the establishment of Buddhism in Japan, but it was to be several years before any real momentum was gained by the Zen Buddhist movement.

Buddhism flourished in the Nara era (710–794) with the help of the ruling classes, and particularly that of Emperor Shomu, with monasteries being founded in all provinces.

During this time several concepts were introduced from mainland China, often through the Korean peninsula, but it was not until decades after the advent of Bodhidharma that the true essence of his teachings gained significant followers in Japan, given the free movement of ideas. One of his followers, Hui-neng (638–713), is known as a key figure in Ch'an's past, since it was he who wrote the Sutra Platform that delineated all of the Ch'an school's main tenets. Many Chinese Ch'an masters came to Japan to spread the Ch'an practice, but they failed to capture a large following even though at the moment there was a great deal of interest in other Buddhist philosophy.

It wasn't until monks Eisai (1141–1215) and Dogen (1200–1253) returned from temples in China from their pilgrimages that Zen began to attract Japanese attention.

Eisai, who had become deeply disillusioned with his native temples ' lack of discipline and growing hypocrisy, set sail for China to learn from the Ch'an masters firsthand. Following numerous stays on two different journeys at Tendai monasteries, Eisai eventually returned to Kyoto and promoted Zen's Chinese style. This was not well accepted by the existing monks, who had friends in high places, and Eisai was forced to travel to Kamakura, the location of the newly established shogunate, where he enjoyed a warm welcome and became the founding abbot of a new Kenninji monastery. From here he learned a combination of Zen, Tendai, and mystical Buddhism which was to become the foundation of the Rinzai group.

After witnessing enlightenment at the Chinese temple on Mount Tian-tong in 1225, Dogen established the Zen Buddhism Soto sect in 1227. Upon his return to Japan, he threatened to ruffle the feathers of the community monks at the Tendai center with his uncompromising attitude to Zen instruction and hard-line avocation of the zazen (sitting meditation) concepts. Disapproving of the political tensions in Kyoto's capital, he transferred his headquarters to the province of Echizen, now Fukui, and founded Daibutsuji that later became known as Eiheiji. Since then, this has become the Soto Zen centre.

While Dogen saw no distinction between the various Zen schools, there were others who categorized them according to the training methods. The Rinzai sect acknowledged the value of zazen but also urged acolytes to expend their emotional effort by reflecting on a koan— an almost irresolvable riddle with no rational responses. The aim was to enable the koan complete the mental process in order to give itself a better view of reality.

Thus, what is Zen?

Ch'an, or Zen, as is more commonly known in the West, is the unusual Chinese way to achieve the Buddhist aim of breaking down all the world's accumulated beliefs to see the world as it is — that is, a mind clear of associations or assumptions. This condition is attained by intense mental effort, and the road is paved by mushin accomplishment (literally "no heart"), where one is released from earthly obligations or wishes. When an emissary learns to relax his thoughts and emotions, then he is able to perceive the world without any preconceived notions. This is the condition for the satori recognized as the state of enlightenment— the aim to which all Buddhists strive. Yes, it is a state of mind that considerable efforts have been made by mystics, sages, and sorcerers to accomplish. Zen varies from other Buddhist sects in that it assumes that knowledge does not arrive slowly, but as a flash of insight, so it does not place much importance on theorizing or attempting to explain the mysterious. This focuses all of its energy on bringing about this monumental shift in consciousness, the shift that will liberate the acolyte from the chains of too concrete an environment.

Because of this, Zen monks became renowned for their erratic behavior and enigmatic responses to questions. We are pretending because our purpose is the greatest source of confusion because it in turn hinders the deeper understanding of the world that occurs beyond language. Human beings are hostages to words and to the meaning that they create.

In many religions and philosophies fracturing the chains of dualism has been an ever-present theme. From the moment we are born, our parents constantly give us a dualistic view of the world, and this is compounded by all those with whom we come into contact until it becomes so internalized that we overlook that it has even been taught. We are told that we are different from the outside environment, and we are separate from things that are not part of our bodies. Zen teachers believe this is mere delusion, and that we are what we feel.

In contemporary psychological terms, when an infant has failed to differentiate himself from the universe he perceives, he is said to become egocentric. It is just this mastered notion that Zen suggests we need to unlearn, differentiate from our climate. The world takes on a new perspective when we loosen the idea of self, or in Freudian terminology the ego, where true art and imagination will begin.

A philosophy professor may begin his first lecture by thinking about the existence of a chair and all the assumptions that were created to arrive at the concept that the chair is a good, stable and real item. This is something that most Westerners would even think a bit insane to imagine. The chair is of course a strong physical body which exists in its own right. To dispute this would suggest that our deterministic view of the world was false, and that it would be appropriate to reassess the ontological precepts that are so embedded in our thought. In learning and devoting ourselves to research we have left behind the illusions that the universe could contain a little more mystery than we expect. Edgar Allan Poe's poem encapsulates the slavish expectations of a scientific worldview.

Wisdom! True Old Time daughter you are!

What affects with your peering eyes certain things.

Why do you feed on the poet's spirit, Vulture, whose wings are boring facts. Zen would suggest we have closed the door to a more comprehensive view of life by embracing, so absolutely, the empirical view of nature and reducing ourselves to a somewhat simplistic perception of something very remarkable. There is a little irony that now, through the analysis of atomic and astral physics, the research that gave us the Newtonian view of the world has discovered that the environment is far from Newtonian in reality.

A stable substance has yet to be discovered, so physicists now come to realize that matter as we recognize it may not actually exist, but is rather an energy stream. Space, time, and mass are all subjective terms and the perception that the universe has become untenable for the scientific community, too, in gradually becoming a fact. Given these observations, there still seems to be a dogged determination to hang on to the old views of reality, which seem to provide the fragile mind with a fairly comfortable refuge that feels the need to cling on to its worldview.

Zen believes that, before being cognitively grasped, our dualistic view of life implies that whatever we experience passes into our internal filtering processes. For every part of our daily lives we use visual boxes so that we can make sense of our environment and communicate with others.

Nevertheless, through language development, an abstract grasp of reality implies that all that we experience is subject to these mental processes, and so we lose the ability to interpret the environment consciously from early childhood. It is at this point where dualism begins.

Nonetheless, perhaps we can always sense the lost world we had as children in our more natural hands, and it may well be this more intuitive sensation that wabi-sabi art helps to bring out. It can bring us back into communication with our nondualist experience, where the need for language is redundant and art may affect our innermost feelings. Beginning from the Buddhist idea that newborn babies are in an enlightened state, it follows that their views of the universe will vary drastically from those of a person who has developed a whole new way of understanding truth.

CHAPTER THREE: THE SPREAD AND TENETS OF WABI-SABI

The feelings of infancy and the images held in the mind's deepest recesses can be affected by realities that we may knowingly be ignorant of, and it may be this implicit connection with wabi-sabi events that cause the emotional responses that we feel. Through their observations into nature, the Zen monks saw the same link between art and the condition of an evolved child, and used art as a medium to rekindle these ties.

Back to the question of "What is Zen?"The Zen masters ' responses reflect the question's irrational and non-intellectuality. Some of the more common replies are: "Zen" "The clouds in the sky and the water in the bottle" "I don't understand" "The silk fan brings me enough of a calming wind" Zen was commonly practiced in a semimonastic setting where fasting and deep contemplation, along with hard physical work, became fundamental principles for the development of one's mind. Given the temples ' minimal existence, they were perfect fountains for creative endeavours, and Zen monks had created much of the art. Not confined to brush painting, these interests involved calligraphy, martial arts, farming, sculpture, and even tea drinking.

The devoted monks tried to find artistic expression in everything they did in a spirit of calm and resolute resolve and this creativity was then the product of their very concentrated minds. The revered monk Hakuin had a common phrase that meditation was far easier in the middle of action than silent contemplation. All they did for the Zen monks became a mystical mission in which they had to immerse themselves fully, and in doing so they immersed themselves in the action rather than in the perception of the activity of their ego.

The direct approach of Zen and its ability to resist clarification offered a more clear view of nature than a verbal perception of it. Through Zen theory the consciousness should be a window not a mirror, so that the universe is seen consciously and not through the intellect's filters.

The Zen view of the world, as nuanced and unfamiliar as it is to the West, may be defined by the following convictions: We exist under the impression that the environment is dual.

Such belief causes people to stick to the image of themselves and the natural universe that contributes to misery afterwards.

Life is ephemeral and brief, but it is essential to the enjoyment of life to overcome the fear of death.

It is possible to break the bonds of our illusions and understand the true nature of our truth by reflection with great effort. In doing so, it frees us from the pain arising from confusion.

Such existence concepts had a powerful effect on the development of art not only in temples but also in Japanese and Chinese cultures, and the focus of Zen art is a physical manifestation of their values. The drawings appeared to be focused on scenes from the landscape, such as animals, plants, cliffs, and mountains, and were portrayed simply as pictures encapsulating their meaning rather than realistic representations of their reality. The painting was usually done in bursts of creativity, and often in large and dramatic brush strokes, where the artist's dream was immediately transferred to paper with little deliberation or reflection.

Rather than concepts relevant to those perceptions, it concentrated on the direct experience of thought. More often than not, such plays had many aspects that could be described as wabi-sabi, and perhaps one should describe the four wabi-sabi tenets as follows: Everything in the world is in transition, coming or going back to nothing.

The basic truism of impermanence can be expressed and implied through Wabi-sabi art.

The understanding of wabi-sabi words will give rise to a quiet meditation of the transience of all life.

A modern and more realistic outlook can be brought to bear on our existence by appreciating this transience.

When Zen became more popular in Japan during the Muromachi era (1333–1568), its impact on policymakers and artists developed tenaciously, and the principles of his theory, so closely linked to those of wabi-sabi, found expression in the painting arts, No drama, flower arrangement, and of course the tea ceremony.

The Tokugawa shogunate (1603–1867) followed the political turmoil of the Muromachi period, whose chaos was no doubt a significant factor in the spawning of so many creative ideas. The atmosphere of life in Japan changed dramatically after Tokugawa Ieyasu had succeeded in bringing all the various warring factions together under one ruling Government. The Protestant influence, which had established a considerable track record in just a few decades, was seen as a clear threat to life in feudal Japan, and so the shogunate decided to close the boarders of Japan to all but the least foreign exchange. This strategy has been known as sakoku (literally "locked land").

Trade was confined to Nagasaki, and accepted only the Dutch, Koreans and Chinese. Several efforts at spreading Christian values were punished with the death sentence. The Japanese had reached their most stable era and it was a phase of arts and culture unification which had been established during the more turbulent Muromachi period.

It was in this conservative environment that the funding of the government for Buddhism, along with that offered by the more prosperous ruling classes, created a fertile climate for theological learning to be furthered. It was also for the Zen monks, who inspired much of the art created during the Edo era (1603–1867), a time of innovation.

Very often, though, the real Zen spirit was corrupted by the balance of power between those with the resources and those with the spiritual direction. This was no different at all from the tensions over the same time between the clergy and the ruling classes of Europe. And despite this conflict of interests between the various sects competing for political and economic favor, the religious and creative emphasis remained strong, and earlier artistic concepts developed and refined.

In the Muromachi era exponents such as Sen no Rikyu (1522–1591) laid the foundations for wabi-sabi art forms, such as the tea ceremony and flower arrangement, and it was these early developments that generated the creative impetus for the subsequent decades. When time went on, the arts that had been developed mainly for the benefit of the ruling elite gradually found their way into the lower class culture. In doing so, Zen's values and his visionary compañero, wabi-sabi, gained greater influence and acceptance across a wide spectrum of Japanese society. After the passing of Sen no Rikyu, other literary figures such as Hakuin (1686–1769) and Sengai (1751–1837) picked up the baton, whose philosophical views of the world pervaded all facets of their voluminous works, and began to promote the artistic movement in Japan— a trend that was becoming mature for an international audience.

Finally Japan restored its boundaries. And after more than 250 years of isolation, the world was swift to see the beauty so scope of Japan's unique art, and it wasn't long until European impressionists like Monet collected large amounts of woodblock prints and other Japanese design artifacts. Yet due to the large distance between the world's philosophical views, the concepts behind wabi-sabi were not picked up as quickly as the more obviously spectacular pieces of art such as the silk kimonos, intricate screens and weapons. It took more time for the West's awareness of wabi-sabi items to grow as a deeper understanding of its significance and purpose began to flood into Western consciousness slowly.

Throughout the last century, a massive exchange of ideas and philosophies emerged in the wake of Japan's rapid unification with the West, with the West being as inspired by Zen as the Japanese were affected by the Western lifestyle. Nevertheless, people's evolving expectations in the modern world have taken their toll on Zen's essence, and particularly in Japan, its importance and ability to influence–as Japanese lives have been slowly subsiding over the past few decades. Yet interestingly enough, as the Japanese seem to leave their religious heritage for Western practiced material hedonism, there is growing interest in the West for the spiritual values inherent in Zen. Interestingly, Zen's potential existence and its art symbol, wabi-sabi, may well reside outside of Japan, and it is the increasing disillusionment of the West with the empty promises of materialism that can provide the requisite catalyst for Zen's widespread adoption of knowledge. The West, which potentially began to dismantle Zen's philosophy, may well hold the key to their future survival.

CHAPTER FOUR: THE WABI-SABI TEA CEREMONY

A glance at the tea ceremony, as the guiding force behind wabi-sabi aesthetics, will shed light on the motives for its creation and the figures that shaped the concepts that remain until today.

"Tea has become more than an idealization of the drinking form; it is the practice of living faith. The beverage developed to be an excuse for the worship of innocence and perfection, a holy activity in which the host and visitor joined together to create the highest beatitude of the earthly for that occasion." – Okakura Tenshin.

For wabi-sabi, the Tearoom is what the chapel is to Catholicism.

All enshrine their beliefs and values, and create an environment conducive to the aims of faith. In a church there is a feeling of respect for the deity of God and His son Jesus Christ; there is a glorification of God's glory and omnipotence within the vaulted ceilings and the beautiful stained-glass photos. There is a stern veneration in the tearoom for undecorated gentility, for the beauty to be contained in the pure and plain most reserved speech. The thought of swapping places triggers some intriguing images.

The tea ceremony, normally held in a secluded and private tearoom, was one of the focal points for wabi-sabi supporters.

It was by this semireligious rite that the tea masters, well versed in Zen's ideology, gave their love of art rich in wabi-sabi language a full voice. They designed their shrines in the same way as ecclesiastical designs have been produced by church clergy. Both are motivated by their own personal beliefs.

The tea ceremony, where wabi-sabi's art and theory cemented its basis, may trace its origins back to China in the twelfth century with Zen monks drinking tea, who assembled before Bodhidharma's portrait and drank the liquid as part of the ritual. As her guiding philosophy, Buddhism, tea love through the Zen monks found its way to Japan. However unlike China, whose sophisticated civilization was decimated by the Mongolian attack in the thirteenth century, Japan was able to continue the refinement of tea drinking until it became an official formal ritual under the patronage of the shogun Ashikaga Yoshimasa.

Japan's elite had a great interest in tea, and it wasn't too long before it had developed itself as a prized beverage to be consumed in a sophisticated climate. The formalization of the tea ceremony began to emerge through the Kamakura era (1185–1333), and certain laws and protocol concerning its use were followed. The tea ritual was embraced along with Zen's beliefs, and the two traditions in Japan formed hand in hand. With the Zen's confidence in grandeur in the smallest things, tremendous emphasis was placed on all the little details of life and care came for attention to detail, and the meditative quality of the tea ceremony came with care. The deep attention required to conduct a tea ceremony was both a practice and a purification, for the remainder of life's problems would melt away through the concentrating of the mind on the tearoom's microcosm.

In the turbulent Muromachi era, the samurai and warrior groups found great relief in the glorious world of tea, when the warring clans both sought to establish greater strength in their power bases. They were existentially separated from their roles and responsibilities as they reached the small room, from the struggles of war, and brought to a position of harmony and peace where the universe could again make sense. As with the creation through history of many great artistic accomplishments, it was the turmoil of the Muromachi era that brought the Herculean leap in Japanese arts. Interestingly, the best art was created under the greatest difficulty, and it was during this period, along with many other peculiarly Japanese art forms, that the foundations for the tea ceremony were established.

The Zen monk Ikkyu (1394–1481) was a seminal figure both in Buddhism and in the creation of a wabi-sabi-style tea ceremony, whose career straddled a period of great political turmoil.

Ikkyu was believed to be Emperor Go-Matsu's illegitimate child and a Kyoto court lady, but after his birth his political abilities caused him several critics, and he and his mother were kicked out of the palace. After that, Ikkyu entered the Ankokuji Zen shrine, where he received extensive instruction in Japanese and Chinese arts and classics. It was more than evident from an early age that he had an incredibly sharp humor, and stories of his exploits still survive today. One of the temple abbots had a great fondness for a sweet snack, which he jealously held in his rooms, and he advised the young acolytes that it was harmful to them.

Unfortunately for the abbot, this did not take in the young Ikkyu, so he purposely destroyed a piece of pottery in the abbot's quarters having shared the reward with his friends. When the abbot returned from his duty, the young Ikkyu clarified that he accidentally broke one of the pots of the abbot and tried to make amends by committing suicide by eating the poisonous candy. Having experienced no ill effect after the first slice he decided it was completely necessary to make sure by consuming them all. His lies and arrogance were revealed, the abbot was in no position to give young Ikkyu an example.

Invited to an audience with the Shogun Yoshimitsu, Ikkyu's impish personality was not even controlled, and when asked if he could capture a tiger, Ikkyu said he could. The shogun then wryly told Ikkyu to use a string he provided on one of the screens to capture the tiger painted on. The young monk leapt into line in front of the mirror without a moment's hesitation, and told the shogun to drive the tiger away.

Despite his obvious laughter, underneath the surface there was a very inspired and genuine Zen practitioner who in his lifetime had an intense urge to achieve true wisdom. He quickly becomes disillusioned with the hypocrisy prevailing in temple life, and at that time the following essay, which he wrote as he left the temple, captured his mood.

Feeling like remorse, no more Zen teachings are being absorbed by triumphant evil forces I will remain silent.

The monks are expected to preach on Zen, but they just talk about their family history. He chose to continue his study with a reclusive monk named Ken'o, who resided in the hills near Kyoto and whose lessons resonated with the authenticity and clarity Ikkyu pursued. Ikkyu served Ken'o diligently, whom he loved intensely, and was so saddened by the death of his lord four years later, that he tried to drown himself in Lake Biwa. His effort was foiled by a servant of his mother who was sent to keep an eye on the despondent young monk. Upon learning under the strict regime of another teacher named Kaso for a few years, he was given a highly prized inka— a diploma from his master that validated his enlightenment. Ikkyu hurled the inka back at his lord and cut himself off as an abbot in another monastery from a potentially lucrative existence. Ikkyu did not put a store of paper enlightenment or the respect it was able to confer — his eyes were set for nothing less than complete freedom. After a subsequent breakdown in their strained relationship, Ikkyu started his trip as an itinerant monk roaming the streets of Kyoto and never really settled for the fifty-five years of his life that remained.

His somewhat odd conduct and quick wit endeavored him to the city's wealthier inhabitants and allowed him to experience some of Kyoto's most sensual delights, including those of the "Floating City." Ikkyu was quite unique in his free use of and apparent enjoyment derived from time spent with female sex, and instead of denying the fact he promoted it as a healthy activity for men and women.

Ikkyu embraced the tea ceremony in his love of life and contempt for formality and laws, and even went so far as to say that it may be more successful than hours spent in solitary contemplation.

With his Zen sense of modesty he moved the tea ceremony's focus away from ostentatious displays of riches and towards the sacred unity of two or more individuals who could meditate on the nature and transience of life in a state of calm and controlled abandonment. While Sen no Rikyu is often regarded as the founder of the tea ceremony, Ikkyu was at the instigation of many of the original ideas and the introduction of rustic utensils. His impact on the tea spirit was far-reaching, and possibly as significant as Sen no Rikyu's later contribution.

It was a pupil of Ikkyu, Murata Shuko (1422–1502), who was to become the Shogun Yoshimasa's tea master. In keeping with the dictums of his father, Shuko had advised the nobility to withdraw from opulence, and instead to concentrate on the personal nature of the human-to-other relationship. It was at this period that inside the Silver Pavillion (Ginkakuji) the first four-and - a-half tatami mat tearoom (each mat being around six foot by three feet) was made.

Ikkyu's dedication to uphold Zen's pure spirit had a major influence on the many facets of his time's art, and it is appropriate that a hanging scroll of his calligraphy was put inside his disciple's first tearoom layout. This then set in motion the Japanese tradition of getting a hanging scroll in the tearoom, from where it became a significant architectural element to be included in many homes across the land — one that is still seen in many houses today.

The Zen philosophy had grown hand in hand with the inspirational arts. It was Takeno Joo who, obtaining tea training from Shuko and Jotei (Ikkyu's trustworthy son), then passed on his lessons to Sen no Rikyu.

Sen no Rikyu's preference for artistic harmony and his predilection for the elegant and unadorned helped shift the focus of the tea ceremony from a show of tradition and riches to a fellowship of kindred spirits searching pure and real. While he suffered an untimely death with the order of his father for ritual suicide, his influence on the arts and the way Zen was used in the arts was a monumental achievement that influenced the Japanese throughout the centuries to come.

It was Zen's power that spread the concepts of silent colours, plain utensils, and simplicity of speech, but it was Rikyu who succeeded in crystallizing these ideas into an esthetic whole and turning the greenhouse, the tea room, fruit, water, and interaction into the sophisticated art form it is now. The tearoom style was an expression of the ideals of Zen temple architecture, with a focus on harmony and sobriety. For the tourist, the little frail hut is a temporary refuge, as the body is but a temporary refuge for the spirit.

For Rikyu came a more established template for the tea ceremony, and according to the instructions of the day's tea master, those rules were set. Many of the theories laid down five hundred years ago have persisted largely intact right up to the present day.

The Tea Ceremony Experience The Tea Ceremony is a multilayered experience in which a person will sample the tastes of carefully prepared foods and drinks in a state of awareness heightened by the tearoom's nurturing environment. The tea ceremony experience is then based in part on the aesthetic pleasure evoked by the tearoom design's wabi-sabi components.

Much about the ritual has been published, with views varying from rapture to an unrivaled ennui. The idealized depiction of a tea ceremony, which might be a distant relative of the modern equivalent, that run along the lines below.

The tea master will agree on a date for a tea ceremony and then pick and welcome a small group of participants whose role and roles would be properly matched, with the utmost care.

The date may well correspond with an upcoming natural event such as the cherry trees blooming, or the autumn leaves' changing colors. He would then make a theme for the machia, or conference, depending on the season and any existing moods, so that the event is held together by the adhesive of continuity.

The tea master must show his readiness to the guests by wetting the stepping-stones near the entrance once all the arrangements are finished. On arrival, the guests must wait in a special room named the machiaishitsu and will have an opportunity to get to know each other and discuss the order in which they will be involved. Since thoroughly cleaning the tea room and placing all the decorative decorations in order, the tea master will then ask the guests to walk through the garden to the tiny tea room.

When passing through the broken stepping stones intended to lead the tourist through the garden's special features, the participants will brace themselves mentally — a training to leave behind themselves and their separate worlds to become one with tea communion. The tenacious moss sticking to the surfaces of the moist cliffs, which seem so alive with a multitude of delicate colours, the streaming of spring water through rustic bamboo into an ancient water bowl, the maple leaves ' vivid autumn colors — all welcome the soul to surrender itself to the unrivaled elegance and natural imperfection of the flickering universe. The trained mind, the guests then walk through the tiny door that symbolizes complete equality in rank and is greeted by the scent of the purest incense as they reach the tearoom's womb.

Within the tokonoma, or alcove, under a kakejiku, or hanging book, lies a perfectly balanced and austerely plain flower arrangement — the flowers representing the kakejiku's feelings. The emotions in the scroll in effect will be a poetic allusion to the conference theme and the guests will love the script's significance and the contrast the bold black ink creates against the light backdrop.

Once all the arrangements are in order, the tea master can now use his consummate expertise to greet the visitors appropriately and serve them food and drinks. Each of the master's movements is pure poetry because its focus adds fluidity and clarity to every movement. The years of practice now put the movements, so often rehearsed, into the domain of art in its purest form, for it is art without meaning, art without feeling, art as a pure link to the ultimate reality.

The master's complete clarity of mind and smooth movements invoke a hypnotic effect in the learners, who can then become one with the tea master's mind and spirit. Here is the paradise and oblivion desired upon earth— the greedy mind that watches our every thought and action, relinquishes its vice-like grasp, and enables us to experience the truth of the present, the eternal, the wondrous, and amazing universe that we all left in our early childhood.

CHAPTER FIVE: THE HISTORY OF SEN NO RIKYU

Sen no Rikyu was born into a fish wholesaler's family in Sakai, though it's claimed his grandfather was a retainer for the Muromachi shogunate. In addition to learning the ritual, he also spent many years at Daitokuji temple in Kyoto as a Zen monk, and it was this experience that influenced his creative work throughout the rest of his long life.

As Rikyu took up Toyotomi Hide-yoshi's place as tea master, he brought the ritual to a new level of sophistication. The tea ritual at the time he began serving his lord was a pastime for the wealthy elite, often an excuse for those of wealth and power to display their friends the ornate and beautifully crafted tea utensils they had purchased from China. By the time he died he had realigned the tea ceremony as an easy and pure process to be celebrated by all.

For Sen no Rikyu this reverence for the great Chinese art works ran contrary to the true spirit of tea. He believed that the attendants and host, by dwelling on the material world, were completely missing the ceremony's hidden meaning, the nature of which rested in its reverence of the humble and ordinary.

The tale has it that one day Sen no Rikyu saw a rustic roof tile whose rugged texture and delicate complexity of color captured his attention as he walked through the area. He requested Chojiro, the roof tile manufacturer, to create some utensils in the same pattern for use in his tea ceremony. Ikkyu had also promoted this introduction of rustic utensils, but with the impact of Rikyu in matters of taste, the relatively small utensil change heralded a monumental shift in the tea paradigm. It was guided away from it, through introspection and a meditation of the evanescence of creation, rather than the subconscious being pulled into materiality. From that time on, Sen no Rikyu tried to reconcile the tea theory more with that of Buddhism, and thereby helped guide the tea ceremony into a more spiritual realm. He took the wabi-sabi ideas, and made them an essential part of the tea ceremony. With that, the use of artistic concepts of wabi-sabi was de rigueur in the tea region. Sen no Rikyu managed to bring the philosophies of tea and wabi-sabi under the same roof and further stressed the importance that could be found in the plain and ordinary.

His conceptual proposals for the tearoom architecture were influenced by the plain and relaxed Zen temple designs. At every step he tried to isolate all that was not simply necessary to leave only the most austere and sublimely elegant atmosphere to enjoy tea sharing.

It was at this time that the concepts of wabi and sabi began to take on far more positive connotations, and the loneliness and isolation of the life of the hermit became associated with freedom from earthly relations. Sen no Rikyu put these wabi-sabi emotions into the architecture of his tearooms so that those who visit will sense the contact of destiny, the movement of life to death, and the serene desolation that arises from this awareness.

Although cleanliness and attention to detail were essential pillars of the tea ceremony, Sen no Rikyu did not want the atmosphere to be sterilized.

There's an anecdote about how he was telling his friend to clean up the area around the tearoom. It consumed most of the day, and then his wife complained that the walking stones were scrubbed three times, the tile was cleaned, and every twig and leaf was picked up. Rikyu then walked over to a maple tree with an autumn leaf that was crimson and shook it so that some of the colorful leaves dropped unexpectedly to the table. He let the beauty of nature put the finishing touches on his son's ambitious efforts, and found a fine balance between the two in doing so. Wabi-sabi is not the work done by nature alone nor is it the work done by man alone. It is a symbiosis between the two. The Japanese also reference this tale as being the best way to describe the wabi-sabi spirit. Wabi-sabi can prevail in nature, but man can only get himself closer to the mysteries that nature hides by capturing its subtlest moods and framing them.

Throughout his seventy years of life, Sen no Rikyu founded himself as the authority of the country on matters of taste and aesthetics, and it is no exaggeration to say that he is the father of what has become the Japanese aesthetic ideal, for he has played a leading role in advancing the wabi-sabi ideals based on tea.

Sadly his presence was not confined to the tea world and his role and power in the political arena caused him to get entangled in the day's chaos. There are several interpretations of why his father, Hideyoshi, forced him to commit suicide, including suspected racketeering of tea utensils, planting his own statue in the shogun's yard, declining to let his daughter marry the son of the shogun. But the most likely reason was that a political enemy had suspected him of plotting to overthrow the shogun grounds adequate to cement his fate.

It was deemed an achievement to be allowed to kill oneself rather than be put to the sword by those of samurai rank or higher. It was seen as far more noble to take one's own life, as one could demonstrate one's aversion to death — one of the gauntlets that Zen had thrown down. The word harakiri (literally "abdomen cut") was important because the stomach was believed to be the place where the soul lives, and thus was the core of a person's will. Rikyu was given this privilege, being of high rank, and Sen no Rikyu conducted a final tea ceremony with his closest friends, in accordance with his values and enjoyment of tea. His commitment and attention to detail had been outstanding throughout the delicate ceremony. After the service, after the tea had been drunk, Rikyu offered his precious tea utensils to his mates, all but his own; these he ground into his mouth, stating, "These cup, stained with the lips of misery, will no longer be used by anyone." Many participating fought back their tears before being asked to leave, while his favored second remained behind to support his master on. Sen no Rikyu then stripped his outer kimono to expose the pure white robe of death that had been carefully hidden underneath, and then, with his last poem of death, he faced his fate in the same stubborn fashion that he had lived his career.

"Come to Thee, O sword of heaven, By Buddha And Through Dharuma Thou hast cleft Thy path."

CHAPTER SIX: ETYMOLOGY OF WABI-SABI

This chapter would examine the etymology of the two terms to illustrate the meaning and confusion they have come to represent, and a broader picture of the emotions the words evoke in the hearts of the Japanese will arise from looking at their use and use through history.

Like many other words describing feelings and philosophies, the phrases wabi and sabi have passed through a century of cultural change, accumulating a vast amount of cultural baggage in this process. The color and complexity of the terms will increase exponentially as context and expected definitions shift. Some of the terms that have been embraced by recent generations, such as hip, evil, and obese, have all taken on optimistic new connotations and have thus modified their definitions. Words are like living organisms, they grow to match the communication needs of those who use a phrase. As the words wabi and sabi have developed over such a prolonged period, they have been used to describe a vast array of ideas and emotions, and therefore their interpretations are more accessible to personal interpretation than almost every other term in the Japanese language.

One of the main reasons the Japanese are never willing to voice a definitive opinion on wabi-sabi is due to the enormous combination of feelings suggested by the word. The Japanese enjoy uncertainty, and the writer should strive, in writing, to optimize the possible significance of his prose by deliberately leaving out subjects and objects, thereby growing the reach of understanding. This is demonstrated very well by three-line haiku poems which open up an idea for the reader to extend as they wish. Rather than trying to define a word, the Japanese prefer to keep the vagueness it reflects. The orientations of those in East and West here show a clear divide. Although Asians tend to prefer instincts and decision-making based on emotion, there is an inherent desire for consistency and rationality in the West that goes hand in hand with the deference of facts. These inequalities also lead to misunderstandings in the discussions between the two.

Zen Buddhists have always been suspicious of language's dangers, and see it as the greatest obstacle to real understanding. The term Furyu monji (literally "not standing on words or letters") reflects the Zen idea that no profound insight can be conveyed by the spoken word: "Those who don't know say, those who don't know talk." Trying to explain the path to enlightenment is as pointless as trying to catch the moon's reflection in a pond, and there is a Zen practice of retaining uncertainty, so that the path to enlightenment is as meaningless as trying to capture the moon's reflection in a pond.

Nevertheless, as people who experience the same range of emotions and face the riddles of life, a commonality of feelings exists within us beyond any culturally biased empirical grasp of reality. It is to these emotional emotions that wabi-sabi is better suited to, and even those with little access to the Japanese arts will find inspiration in the simplicity of wabi-sabi and the values it reflects while resisting too much analytical study. While it may be unattainable to understand the term within a solely Japanese context, the essence of the concept that it enshrines is there for everyone to appreciate.

The wabi-sabi knowledge can be strengthened by gazing at the forms in which the two terms have developed over the years.

The term wabi derives from the verb wabu, meaning to languish, and the suffix wabishii, used to define feelings of loneliness, forlornness and suffering. Nevertheless, the literati of the Kamakura and Muromachi eras used those somewhat negative connotations in a much more positive way to express an existence that was freed from the material world. A life in hardship was the Zen model for a monk pursuing the ultimate truth of nature and so the romantic vision of a man who transcended the need for the comforts of the physical world and managed to find peace and harmony in the simplest of lives emerged from these negative images.

In a literary sense, one of the first references to the term sabi was created by the poet Fujiwara No Toshinari, who used it to convey a sense of desolation, using such visual images as frost-wiped reeds. This trend of use grew, as did the sense of absolute isolation and ultimacy suggested by the word, and it went hand in hand with the Buddhist concept of the eternal transience of existence known as mujo. Taken from the Sanskrit anitya meaning transience or mutability, the idea of mujo shapes the axis around which Zen theory orbits, and has long been intertwined with the doctrines of the Japanese artistic community. The belief that nothing remains unchanged and that all sentient beings will perish has always provided the finishing touch and gives meaning to all human actions. Death's contact is seen as the best possible source of wisdom, for when the thought of not living is put into the mix nothing can seem more relevant than anything else. There is an obsession with death within the Japanese, and unlike the West, which appears to shy away from what could be perceived as grim debates, the Japanese try to use the emotional effect of death to bring strength and power to their acts. With this force comes also a feeling of inconsolable desolation, and the word sabi is often related to this emotion. The word sabi was employed by the great haiku poet Matsuo Basho (1644–1684) as an esthetic juxtaposition to the essence of life and based on the impermanence of our condition and the stupidity of attempting to deny this unmoving reality. Nevertheless, the elegance of Basho's writing focused on the negative aspects of old age, loneliness and mortality and imbued them with a serene sense of beauty.

Melancholy, an emotion nurtured in the Zen community, was used as a whetstone for sharpening spiritual awareness; it was not a self-indulgent self-pity type, but rather a sorrow tinged with an elusive longing. It was in the midst of the most hideous of human conditions that real beauty could be discovered and when our lives are put into context, the bonds of the unconscious mind, so aware of our fragility, can be struck so profoundly. Some, like the great Zen scholar Daisetz Suzuki, say it's just a mere sense of truth that we left as infants, the environment of the here and now, untouched by language or beliefs. It is a reality that is submitted to the realm of philosophy at some stage in everybody's childhood— an environment that is being continually interpreted and clarified by logical machinations, a future that is no longer in direct contact with the present.

So the words wabi and sabi both have their origins in the universal Zen nihilist vision and express the interplay of youth and old age, elegance and ugliness, existence and death — nature cycles. If one wishes to be more descriptive, wabi appears to be more closely associated with lifestyle, while sabi is often used to characterize the more physical characteristics of items that show a sense of the impermanent, astringent and unpretentious in nature. This being said, the terms have acquired so many connotations and meanings that the two can be used interchangeably and together for all intents and purposes, at least in academic circles. The significance inferred by any of the three variations reflects something so immense and elusive that further grouping in scholastics goes against the Zen spirit.

The wabi-sabi aesthetic principles, though, used not only in the tea ceremony but in almost any aspect of Japanese artistic expression, have come to represent a link between the trappings of the material world and the tug we all experience, to a greater or lesser degree, into a life of poverty and simplicity. If the spirit is ready and willing, then a three-line haiku poem set in the tokonoma (the standard alcove), complemented by a plain but perfectly balanced flower arrangement, will serve to drive the viewer's consciousness to new heights and help him or her find a serene equilibrium between the joy of life and the inevitability of the waiting gap.

As with all forms of art, it is the audience's mental experience which will determine the interpretation result. The charm seen in the opening of a single bud or the patina of an antique bamboo vase will be far more evocative for the Japanese, who have a long tradition of spiritual discipline and an admiration for exquisite simplicity than a symbol of riches, strength or opulence.

The above, however, without wanting to limit the meaning of the word wabi-sabi, constitutes a personal interpretation which can only serve as a starting point for the future inferred.

Wabi-sabi is an intuitive appreciation in the physical world of a timeless beauty that represents the eternal flow of existence in the spiritual world. It is an understated elegance that resides in the humble, rustic, unfinished, or even decayed, an aesthetic sensibility that sees in the impermanence of all life a melancholic beauty.

When the tea masters of old Zen were asked to explain the principles of wabi-sabi, they declined to offer a definitive version in true Zen form, but instead cited the following poem by Fujiwara no Sadaie, which is said to capture the spirit of wabi-sabi: Looking far ahead, I see no cherry trees, nor tinted leaves: only a small hut on the sea, In the dusk of an autumn night.

There's still a noticeable reluctance for the Japanese of today to adhere to any commonly accepted meaning as such. The traditional Japanese tolerance of uncertainty and fondness also helped preserve and develop the very unique atmosphere that surrounds wabi-sabi.

It is the very fact that it cannot be described that makes it so special and sacred, and wabi-sabi owes much for its continued survival to this Japanese characteristic.

CHAPTER SEVEN: THE EFFECT OF WABI-SABI ON JAPANESE LIFESTYLES

Although stereotypes also downplay individuals within a community, they do provide patterns in attitudes and behaviors to sociologists that enable for comparisons between cultural groups. As German designs represent commonly held attitudes about quality and reflects Bauhaus-enced culture of speech, so wabi-sabi is a consequence of cultural values in Japan. A look at the citizens of Japan may demonstrate how their social values have come to represent this style of art.

The Japanese culture has come under the microscope on many times as one of the countries most geographically and culturally homogenous groups of people. As with her literature, though, Japan shows a passion for the mysterious and ambiguous, and this ancient tradition of subtlety has become evident in her actions in the seemingly irreconcilable contradictions. Wabi-sabi's Japanese cultural vision is the product of their propensity for the enigmatic, and as with all many societies, a country's creative production is a mirror image of the prejudices the typify that community.

Similarly, Japanese enjoy art that provides great room for compromise and a degree of uncertainty, they often favor a non-cemented dialogue of definitive statements or negations. Throughout her culture, the institutional structures are the product of both the patriarchal tradition and the Zen teachings that have become assimilated into the national psyche.

The Japanese people would rarely allow themselves to be dragged into a philosophical discussion, but their cultural values provide some of the strongest and most clear observations into reality — they practice their ideology rather than analyze it. In the West there is a propensity to hypothesize and evaluate, but not to lead lives which support the hypotheses.

Philosophers, as "Kierkegaard" figured out, make wonderful palaces but then live next door in the shed.

On a national character, few variables hold more sway than the weather. The temperate climate Japan experiences offers some of the season's most spectacular shifts, and it is to these that the Japanese direct their desires and energy. Blessed with some of the world's most beautiful plants, Japan can be truly breathtaking in fall or spring, and cherry blossoms have become one of the Japanese calendar's defining features. Hundreds of thousands of small and large parties are organized under them during the brief time that the millions of cherry trees in Japan are blossoming. Sake is consumed, songs are sung, and the flickering charm of the blossoms is thoroughly appreciated. They are cherished in the confidence of being able to withdraw their glory at a moment's notice at the whim of wind or rain itself.

It is like a celebration of our own transient existence, and another means for the Japanese to indulge in their impermanent enjoyment of life.

Seasonal change has always been a recurring theme in the art of Japan, and is often used to illustrate our own passage of time. Spring, for example, is often used for the erotic stage of life as an euphemism (the term prostitute is actually made of the 3 characters "selling spring woman"). But fall and winter are associated with the latter years of life and are used extensively in the language of poetry and authors (the word autumn fan is a way to refer to a lady who has reached her prime). Often, when food is served, a seasonal leaf or flower is usually placed as a flourish and a sign that everything has its season and they have to be enjoyed. The passage of seasons is a recurring theme in wabi-sabi phrases, and they are often used to evoke emotional reactions.

Despite their passion for silence, the Japanese often tend to keep their feelings relatively tightly hidden. A boss's straight face will mask either love or contempt; it is only the Japanese's lengthy and meticulous social experience that enables understanding of the social codes.

A foreigner who first came to Tokyo could find the lack of emotion shown in public to represent a cold and unin viting human.

The masking of feelings for the Japanese though, is in accordance with the Zen principle of being numb and aloof regardless of the circumstances one sees themself. Sumo wrestlers are normally questioned in one of the big Basho sumo tournaments after a win, but they show complete ignorance, as it would seem arrogant and conceited to seem jubilant. A grin would be horribly frowned upon in this land of ancient traditions, and would indicate the wrestler was under the impression that his victory was significant.

From the many gifts given to express gratitude to the highly complex vocabulary used to display deference and respect, Kenkyo, or humility, occurs frequently in Japanese culture. As a community which for its labor-intensive rice farming had to depend on smooth group dynamics, the Japanese have never been a race to accept those who wish to appear unique or better. Modesty with your fellow men and modesty in the presence of the forces that govern our lives is a much-admired quality of Japanese society, and is continually emphasized in schools and the workplace. Company leaders never receive huge salaries themselves and usually eat in the same canteen as the manual workers. The subtlety of these social interactions stretches even to the width of a bow and to refraining from using the name of an older person.

Just that is what your elder brother is called, your boss is addressed by his job title, and doctors and teachers are all called by the generic sensei term.

It is this modesty for deities, ancestors nature and other humans that has been ingrained in the way an artist or craftsman views himself and his work. For example, a Japanese carpenter will treat his tools and the materials that he uses with intense reverence. The purpose is to do the best to bring out in a harmonious way the inner beauty of the wood. He will not receive recognition or appreciation for the job until his work is done, because he has a deep sense of satisfaction that he has done his best and can't do more. This sense of humility is wabi-sabi's backbone, which prevents artists ' performance from being corrupted by an artist's pretensions or aspirations. Wabi-sabi artwork must have this essential element of modesty to preserve its moral integrity.

Besides this sense of humility, there's another reason the Japanese maintain the smooth flow of social interaction. The words tatemae and honne are viewed as the cornerstones of social lubrication while rejecting Japanese social behaviours. The tatemae is the mask that one reveals to society, the face that one is expected to show to society, but the honne is one's true heart, and one that often has to be closely veiled for the sake of maintaining social order. It may seem insincere or even unethical to some international outsiders, but the basic principles for the unspoken way of behaving are for the People. The rules are known by all because of the complicity in the game and the indications read very plainly, whereas a foreign observer might miss them completely.

Such lack of association with the Japanese Culture Club makes it extremely difficult for outsiders, however eager they may be to learn the language or protocol, enter into the community and be fully accepted. In comparison, Japanese also often find it difficult to fit comfortably into Western classes, whose structures are regulated by a different set of rules.

There is no question that the mysterious Japanese personality that took them through one of the most fascinating periods in the world will continue to taunt and annoy those in the West who are trying too hard to examine and appreciate it. Like the French of Europe, the Japanese feel that they have a very sophisticated national, culinary and cultural background, although they can be a little more reserved in their beliefs, unlike the French. How they think is not the same, honne, and what they claim in public, tatemae.

Refinement and dishonesty travel a very narrow line, but as insulting others would be far worse, the most appropriate course of action is that which would maintain the status quo, and that is why the Japanese are such exemplary hosts. Anybody who is fortunate enough to cross the threshold into a household in Japan will attest to the hosts' unnerving ability to discern their needs and moods. The clues offered by the Japanese are so precise that their interpretation of circumstances is finely tuned, so when foreigners join the picture, their moods and are often well expected, used to years of more direct communication.

Through their attention to their art appreciation, Japan's openness to social occasions is reflected. They stand with the elusive and mysterious and their social makeup's nuances go hand in hand with the nuances of their love for art. Wabi-sabi provides a great outlet for the season-aware Japanese to find a subdued yet passionate platform for their social and artistic tastes.

When we step into the twenty-first century, Japanese social norms are evolving at a pace beyond precedent. Such shifts in the structure of the society of Japan have a dramatic effect on the national identity and thus their attitudes regarding art and design.

As seen in movies and commercials, the youngsters of Japan have become very comfortable with Western values, and now there is a noticeable swing away from more traditional values. The room given to wabi-sabi is definitely diminishing within the frenetic and chaotic urban lifestyle, and its potential importance in contemporary Japan is under pressure.

For many centuries, Zen and wabi-sabi have been the predominant pillars of Japanese artistic endeavors, but since the pressures of modern life have forced a change in art and design standards, Japanese society's nature has also experienced a radical change in principles.

The rather unimpressed journalist, Alex Kerr, who had lived in Japan for decades, was of the opinion in his book "Lost Japan" that from being one of the most beautiful countries in the world when he first arrived, Japan had turned itself into one of the most physically unattractive countries. For a nation that has fostered such a strong aesthetic ideal, is Japan now breaking ties with its cultural heritage and allowing the wabi-sabi aesthetics to languish in art history annals?

Those who claim that the death of this esthetic value is all but complete can quote the modern art that occupies most urban skylines, demonstrating a surprising lack of restraint over the last 50 years. The Japanese curiosity in Western items has been almost insatiable since the fall of the Tokugawa shogunate in the latter half of the nineteenth century, spanning from the trendy top hats of the nineteenth century to McDonald's modern-day food creations and associates. A journey to the heart of Tokyo from the extremely futuristic Narita airport will not offer much in the way of visual pleasure, as the tangle of highways, overhead power lines and houses sprawl together in no manner that enticing. The views given once in town are not much of an upgrade, and a visit to a Japanese family house would probably dissipate any preconceived notions of the traditional home with its simplicity and minimalistic space. Most of the houses or apartments in the densely populated cities are packed with modern furniture, household appliances and clean storage facilities.

Unfortunately, the shortage of elegance in urban areas is not restricted to the domestic scene and Japan may be justifiably suspected of spawning some of the most indescribably awful design. An indication of this is the vast array of "love hotels" whose architectural trends involve oddities such as mosques in the Aladdin style and a replica of the QE2 ocean liner. Such hotels, which provide rooms for "over-night visits" and "one-hour rests," have flourished due to the difficulty of seeking privacy in the paper wall property.

The pachinko parlor is another Japanese artistic disaster that one could say is the direct opposite of wabi-sabi. Pachinko is a type of vertical bagatelle where ball bearings work their way through pins and gates and can trigger other balls to fall into the bottom of the waiting tray. The aim of the game is to gather as many balls as possible that can be traded for commodities or tokens. Such houses, which can house hundreds of computers, are often tastelessly situated in the middle of beautiful rural scenery accompanied by plenty of flashing pink and purple neon lights; they are glittering, inexpensive, brash, loud, money-oriented dens of iniquity that would make Sen no Rikyu fall into his grave many times.

It is a regrettable but undeniable truth that in modern Japan it is far more difficult to find the artistic and spiritual peaks reached in the days gone by. In addition to fashion, the contemporary tea ceremony has been suspected of becoming religiously vacuous by people including Yanagi Soetsu, a leading figure in Japan's design revolution, who vehemently opposed the so-called high art he saw bringing down the Japanese's whole aesthetic sensibility. The sheer predominance of the material culture and the frenzied nature of modern existence make it hard for tea masters and participants alike to achieve complete abandonment within the tiny tearoom.

In the routine and near-obsessive study of protocol and laws Rikyu's dream of a sacred gathering with kindred spirits has been somewhat lost.

Like with many of the Japanese disciplines, there is a deep deference for all the values laid down by the teachers of yesteryear, and a refusal to move away from the laws passed down from generation to generation, however ritualized and pointless they may have become. The contemporary tea ritual has become a target of this Japanese characteristic, and if some people are unable to drink from the same cup as Rikyu, perhaps this must be due in part to the decay of the art form and its digression away from its roots in ease, honesty, and modesty. As Rikyu said, "The tea ceremony is nothing more than boiling water, steeping tea, and drinking it." Wabi-sabi has very limited significance within the modern lives of urban dwellers, and it is already a foregone conclusion for many of its demise.

This turning away from custom and putting on more modern values and architectural criteria on a full scale gives the impression that Japan has become a wasteland for the arts. But of course there is another side to the story, and with its abundance of natural beauty and peerless social sophistication, Japan is still able to offer some incredible glimpses into the transcendent culture that it has so carefully fostered to those who pursue it.

Tucked away in the back streets of Kyoto, one can consider the Tawaraya Hotel, an oasis for the search of the quintessential definition of Japanese hospitality, a million miles from the "love hotels" and the unchecked urban sprawl. One might be forgiven for not even noticing the low-level building, since there is little outside to suggest the history in it.

The guest is formally welcomed at the front door and the shoesare re-moved and replaced with slippers before the guest is then led to the door containing the personal name of the space by the tight, softly lit wooden floor halls. The kimono-clad hostess then kneels and with consummate elegance slides back the door granting you the first view of your own exquisite organic manifestation. No room, no TV, no bright colors, only a show of extraordinary discipline. Everything sticks out and yet architectural gems, including the toilet, are to be appreciated everywhere. There's a rectangular Japanese wooden bath in lieu of the normal western wash, a luxury that could stretch the strongest will. These are made exclusively from Hinoki (Japanese cypress) without nails or wax and can be airtight for decades to come. While they look wonderful, it is not until you are fully submerged that their full value can be felt, with the smell of the wood lifting up the senses.

Your own little garden is beautifully outlined by a window that makes for just the right view, and the doors take you out into the miniature world that is carefully designed. You have tea and a wash and then you expect the evening meal in a loose fitting yukata (cotton kimono), which is delivered to your space as with most Japanese inns. The cuisine is a real joy for the gourmand as the vast array of flavors and textures are sculpted onto the crafted pottery, creating a seasonal image with the choice of products and the flowers used for decoration. You might be ready to try some calligraphy after a few cups of sake using the given writing kit.

You may feel worn and scuffed by the stresses of the day when you reach the hotel, but when you depart you know your own composure and strength has been returned in the same way as your shoes have been cleaned. The hostess doesn't waste much effort to ensure your stay is an unmatched delight. Each step and every phrase that is said is the result of a mind centered on her art's excellence, and it is in this universe that one can always consider the wabi-sabi spirit alive and really well.

The Tawaraya serves as an everlasting symbol of ancient Japanese culture, but in order to find wabi-sabi in everyday life one does not have to make a special journey to Kyoto. Even in Tokyo's metropolis one is never far from an old temple or garden and the tradition of an alcove with a scroll and flower arrangement is still prevalent in many homes.

While the Japanese embrace new concepts, an enduring devotion to the simple and natural elegance found in wabi-sabi persists.

It's sometimes hard to see how comfortably the Japanese live with their seemingly irreconcilable style contradictions. But Japan has been a land of extraordinary paradoxes throughout its existence, and one wonders if Japan's ability to live with these glaring incongruities might in part be due to its Zen values of nonduality. When attractiveness and ugliness are only two sides of the same coin divided by intellectual activity, then it is not a matter of accepting their coexistence. This may be one of the explanations for the physical development of modern Japan, where a three-tier golf driving range could flank the majestic Kyoto gardens. The Japanese seem to tolerate these obvious confrontations with silent indifference, and as an outsider it is enticing to believe that more should be done to preserve the precious cultural heritage. (Should Hitachi advertisements be permitted within the sanctuary of the Kyoto Garden, even if they provide maintenance sponsorship?) Taking wabi-sabi as an example of Japan's reactive approach to development, it is fair to say that wabi-sabi would be a marginal issue for most people living in modern Japanese cities as a commonly used and discussed issue. When viewed in its historical context, however, it is possible that the relevance of wabi-sabi to modern Japanese is more obvious. Anyone growing up in Japan will come into contact with thousands of pieces of Japanese art, including pottery, poetry, calligraphy, flower arrangements, gardens, temples— the list is nearly endless. These may imply very little in particular, but taken as a whole, they continuously perpetuate the subliminal message implicit in wabi-sabi, and as such will have a driving effect on the visual sensitivities of those in the community. The longer a traveler lives in Japan, the more he is affected by the everyday things he experiences, and the host nation's preferences.

If they asked their view on the subject of wabi-sabi, younger Japanese will possibly shrug and say it is a difficult question. Yet the reality that the younger Japanese of today may not express that wabi-sabi is important simply demonstrates that they are not consciously aware of their cultural influence — ences— not that wabi-sabi's artistic values are no longer relevant to the consciousness of the country. The long historical presence of wabi-sabi and its permeation through the years into almost all Modern art forms has left an indelible mark on the common aesthetic appreciation in Japan. Far from being outdated, it still carries on through this cultural heritage and still plays an important role in how the Japanese decide what pleases the senses, or is not. It is in this unspoken context that the influence of wabi-sabi sensibility often exerts itself on contemporary Japanese people's aesthetic sensibilities.

It lives on in the first Sony Walkman's plain, clean design, in the austere, sober Ando architecture, and in the handmade pottery that is still a part of everyday life. Cynics may have written off wabi-sabi as an ancient form that has long ago stopped affecting contemporary Japanese, but in the love of seasons and a deep understanding of the impermanence of life, they still maintain a profound admiration of wabi-sabi things— an enjoyment that has not changed for a millennium.

CHAPTER EIGHT: WABI-SABI FOR THE CREATIVES

Having looked at the properties of wabi-sabi, we will now move on to ways to use these ideas in modern living. The following section discusses the various materials that can be used and suggests how these elements could be used to enhance the environments in which we spend time.

There are two levels of approach when specifying wabi-sabi. The very ethereal stage where elegance and spirituality combine, and the more realistic point where Zen will direct mere mortals ' creative ambitions. While for most people a perfect philosophical understanding of art and aesthetics is an unrealistic goal, the art of wabi-sabi still has much to offer in modern theory of design.

The whole concept is focused on modesty towards one's own life and the world at large in a purist and very Japanese interpretation of wabi-sabi. This quotation from a Japanese potter puts into context the essence of the wabi-sabi philosophy: "Wabi and sabi are almost impossible to define precisely. Perhaps one would claim its living alone with our fellow men without a desire for profit, rejecting thoughts of self-importance or prestige, and humbly embracing our position in life. "Wabi-sabi is the esthetic that comes naturally from this mentality.

The mentality does not exist in the art. It would be wrong to say that wabi-sabi art can be coerced or replicated because its essence and fleeting existence would be rejected. As our feelings are in constant flux, so is the world we perceive, and for us to catch the fleeting beauty our minds and motivations must be clear and free from the folly that prevails in much of our behavior in the 21st century.

There are no hard-and-fast guidelines on what is and what isn't wabi-sabi for those influenced by the wabi-sabi feelings and the promise it provides. If something evokes feelings of an intangible yearning then for the person concerned something has wabi-sabi. It's very personal and subjective just like all art. However, the Japanese generally agree without recourse to classification or intellectual analysis on what objects, scenes, or other mental stimuli evoke these wabi-sabi sentiments. Using these as a starting point, the following section will examine some of the parameters for wabi-sabi designs that suggest ways to incorporate them into a modern lifestyle.

MATERIAL CHOICE A key factor in creating a wabi-sabi atmosphere is choice of material.

Wabi-sabi's initial exponents promoted the use of natural resources-mud, stone, wood, bamboo, linen, paper, cotton, wheat, and even iron. The intention was to use easy-to-eye fabrics with muted colours, and a tendency to shift visually with time. As most of the combinations were seen in the environment, color and textural combinations were also transplant naturally. Almost all wabi-sabi words need an aspect of the biological, as there is no sense of time and no sense of impermanence without that. Glass, aluminum, and plastic are generally considered inappropriate materials for a true wabi-sabi expression because of their uniform shiny surface and inability to express the impermanence of all matter.

USING WOOD

Japan has had a lasting love affair with wood because it is highly suitable for both functionality and esthetic expression. The tree grows from a seed and eventually reaches the end of its life over the course of a few hundred years and then returns to the soil where other trees will be sustained by its decay. The tree's fight to conquer the environment's persistent powers can be seen in every part of it. The centuries-long struggle for survival is evident in the grains and knots in the branches that have tried to absorb the energy of the sun and the roots that have found moisture and soil stability. There are trees with gnarly barks and unusual forms that reflect some of the most captivating creations of existence, because they are the beauty of imperfection.

Apart from some incredibly resilient woods like teak, most woods will continue their journey back to the nothingness from which they came, even when cut and treated, and in this passing their colors and shades, grains and figures can provide both beauty and utility.

For those involved in using wood to wabi-sabi words, the pieces of wood that have the greatest potential are often the parts that are at their most complex levels of devolution. As the chemical makeup of the cells in the wood varies with the passage of decades, the colors are darker and the defects more prominent, and for that reason many of the most interesting pieces are to be found among the discarded parts in reclamation yards. Oak beams, which for half a millennium held a house roof, bent and contorted as the highest traces of rain began making their way to the surface, provide incredible potential. It is then up to the artist to take the old tree's spirit and frame it in such a way as to do justice to its long voyage.

Cleaning these beams is like an adventure, as the wire brush cuts the years of cumulative grime away to expose the secrets underneath. Once the dirt has been painstakingly removed, the smooth parts can be sanded and polished to provide a finish where there is visual relief between the rough and smooth ones. Using a brushed-on sanding sealer and then a wax coat helps to deliver a patina where the high spots of brightness resemble the feeling of a piece of wood that has been handled for years as gently. For the final finish of the product the patina is absolutely critical as it makes all the difference to the visual impact. The eye is very sensitive to these subtle variations, and every effort must be expended to develop a patina capturing the extended history of the wood for a piece to be really appealing.

Where many Western countries have used stone as their primary building block, the Japanese have traditionally favored wood and paper to counter the extreme climate swings and ever-present earthquake threats. They extensively used wood and paper as walls and room dividers, but unlike other countries the Japanese rarely painted their wood, preferring instead to savor the grain-making figures. This use of timber and other naturally occurring products in the construction process meant that everything remained silent and normal in the interior colours. There was no need to match colors because the nature palette had already matched them perfectly. One of the overriding feelings when visiting a traditional Japanese interior is one of complete unaffectedness and a feeling of unity. Restraint determines the limits once more and multiplies the overall effect.

Upon visiting a typical temple or home, it is impossible not to note the many parts of carefully crafted wood and the attention to detail that has gone into their creation and the elaborate joinery thereof. His work, if that can be called, is meditative for the Japanese carpenter, and becomes an expression of true dedication to craftsmanship. Both his tools and the wood he uses enjoy an unspoken reverence, and a carpenter is said to be able to spend up to a third of his time sharpening his tools so that the cuts he makes are as clean and precise as possible. Each piece of wood is as unique as the tree from which it originated, with its own beauty potential. There is a tendency in the mass production of furniture to remove all the wood that doesn't adhere to the design and only retain the portion that is deemed useful. As a result, the typical cause of the oak board wastage in the U.K. It is more than 50 per cent, but if each item is analyzed for its own value, then much more of the tree's essence could

be conveyed and less of the valuable source
expended.

The great American-born woodworker George Nakashima has built his work around the principle that every piece of wood has a perfect use, and it is up to the woodworker to find that use and let the tree live on through his craft. His research centers on the wood's natural beauty, and works it to give full exposure to the colors and figures that come from the spontaneous flow of wood fibres. If there is a big crack in the wood or a knot, then woodworkers like Nakashima, instead of taking it out, make it a key feature of the board and encourage the people who look at the piece to admire the asymmetry created by the mark of nature. For wood there seems to be a universally shared love of the figures and flows contained within its materials, more than any other media. And the figurative design of a wood such as walnut, with a grain like licorice tentacles spiraling around a circle, will catch a sense of wonder and awe and keep recapturing. Although not specifically named wabi-sabi, Nakashima's furniture and other like-minded woodworkers make no effort to conceal the joy that wood brings to the exquisite imperfections that nature makes. Timber uses: upper flooring. Old character floorboards are perfect, and the strongest boards are frequently found in reclamation yards. For a nice patina the wood must be sanded, sealed and then finished to a perfect finish. Usually the older the wood the stronger and some businesses also sell flooring made from large sections of very old timber, which has obviously deteriorated with age.

Beams and supports revealed. Throughout Japan's tearooms the space is physically separated by both wooden and bamboo struts, and the walls are often filled in on top of the wooden frame's asymmetric design.

Wooden items include cups, vases, tables, driftwood, curious origins, etc. Bowls made from burr woods like oak or elm tend to work well, and in sawmills such burr off-cuts are often usable. In addition, one can take a whole chunk of burr and cut a bowl from the center leaving as it is the outer bark. Many furniture (tables, benches, work tops, shelf units). The waney or natural edges left on boards add a visual softener to the lines and give a more organic feel to the furnishings. A ride to a wood manufacturer that normally makes its own boards out of logs can turn up some very unusual board forms. You can then render the furniture to improve the board's natural shape.

Reclaimed coastal timber furniture located in warehouses, ports and secure seaside regions. Greenheart and other such timbers that have been destroyed by the passage of the sea for years have some exceptionally attractive shapes which can be integrated into interiors or gardens. When producing tables, vases, cups, and the like, they can be cut into more functional sizes; used as decoration parts on their own; or inserted into other furniture designs. Care should be taken with greenheart, as it has an erratic grain impact on devices and an extraordinary blunting effect.

Reclaimed railroad furniture. Like sea protection wood in its deteriorated shape, it can be used in many of the same ways. A basic bench created by taking two parts for the legs, and then using the remainder for a bench top, could be an example. With railroad ties varying from pine treated to teak a wide variety of timbers were used. Untreated hardwoods are more pleasant to work with, and have more appealing patinas typically. Any dust or stones that have become stuck in the forest should also be carefully avoided.

Bamboo interior fitting pieces, greenhouse splitters, vases, candles, etc. There are many different types of bamboo including an attractive black bamboo that can be used instead of poles or curtain rods. It is important to reduce splitting when using bamboo, that it has been well seasoned. Scorching the bamboo with a flame renders the bamboo brighter and can significantly contribute to its visual appeal.

USING METAL

Metals including iron are very sensitive to shifts in corrosion and color, and since they are radically different in look and appearance, they provide a good contrast to the other components used in wabi-sabi that appear more naturally. The iron kettle used in the tea ceremony is an example of how the impermanence of metal's value is stressed and cherished. The slow corrosion on the surface of the metal will become more pronounced with the passing of the years, as will the vast array of subtle hues within the surface. The range of colors this produces and the resulting surface pitting epitomize wabi-sabi, and while the Chinese characters are different, the Japanese word for rust is in fact sabi. Nevertheless, the perfect finish isn't a pure rusted surface alone, as the oranges are too solid. It is the very gradual, unforced color shift that is being pursued, and this is a phase that cannot be rushed around.

One contemporary Japanese artist uses metal sheets made from old ships ' hulls and then removes them to fit with the bits of wooden furniture he creates. The sheets are all carefully cleaned with a wire brush to remove any excess rust and then add protective oil.

Wrought iron and zinc are amongst other metals that lend themselves to a wabi-sabi feel. Wrought iron and cast iron are hard to work but some of the discarded parts have excellent potential for wabi-sabi projects. We have been through the aging process already and have all the color and texture complexity needed for integration into wabi-sabi designs. Before the advent of stainless steel, zinc was used for its non-rusting qualities but it inevitably darkens as it oxidizes over a long period of time, creating a very appealing patina. Conran furniture manufacturers have developed a way to enhance this cycle chemically, and sell tables whose patina has a very wabi-sabi feel.

Metal alone can be a bit tough and loses warmth, but it has a natural affinity to wood. Wood is much easier to work in three dimensions, and there are a great many combinations of the two textures.

Metal uses: rollover furniture (especially wood). Old metal sheets can work fine as shelves. Other pieces can form legs or even tabletops found in metal recycling yards. Quite often a visit to such locations will give inspiration for a piece of furniture and then the wood can be carved to match the metal's qualities.

Industrial reclaimed, nautical or building iron used as part of a functional design. Oddly shaped containers have great potential and can act as a foundation for a candle, a decorative vase or even a fruit bowl.

• Hangings on the mirror. Once placed on a blank wall, heavily corroded sheets of metal with multiple layers of corrosion and vivid textural designs can be very enticing. Often a coat of oil helps bring out the colors and prevent more degradation.

Heat-treated steel shifting color with high temperatures or charcoal burning used as part of a functional design or as a hanging curtain. Interesting patinas will occur on the surface when steel is heated to the high temperatures. There is also a method where charcoal-heated stainless steel produces an attractive black matte finish. When left unrestrained, large flat sheets will be vulnerable to warpage.

Chemically altered metals used in a functional design or as a hanging curtain. Chemical reactions produce marks on a metal surface which are intermittent and spontaneous. This is a quite specialized field but there are several forms in which metals can obtain a surface color to improve their appearance. An innovation rooted in our own design work is a mild steel process where the sheets are chemically blackened and then sanded with a very fine wet and dry sandpaper and lubricating oil. The best markings are formed on the surface at the grinding of the metal sheets, and this becomes noticeable only when the black coating is partly withdrawn. The random nature of the mottled look and the sheet's muted black color served well as a comparison to the more natural types of woods like oak. (See shelving machine illustration.)[Hand-beaten sheet metals instead of utensils]. An example of this could be a 4 mm square sheet of character steel pounded into the form of a bowl (found in a reclamation yard or the like.

USING PAPER

The amount of handmade papers produced in Japan is overwhelming, and the practice extends decades. In the West the persistence of the belief that paper was a means for the processing of knowledge or as a foundation for other forms of artistic expression persisted until more recently. Nevertheless, in the East there has been a long-standing appreciation for the inherent elegance of handmade documents, crafted in a large variety of styles from a variety of natural ingredients.

In 1928 there were no fewer than 28,532 Japanese families involved in the traditional paper making business, which provided the tremendous demand for decorative and architectural purposes.

Created without the use of bleaches or other additives, the papers absorb natural ingredients ' various textural and visual complexities and become a rare and colorful tapestry. The paper's delicacy belies its inherent power and one can notice some very wabi-sabi complexities in this delicacy and randomness of shape. Japanese artists, including Isamu Noguchi, have long abused the properties of paper, the innovative lamp designs of which have become a well-known feature of homes around the world. The lightness and translucence of paper, coupled with its ease of molding, gives artists the opportunity to exploit this economic resource in a variety of ways.

Such paper properties are used in the making of shoji, or windows, which require only enough light to reach in the tearoom, but ensure it is diffused and unobtrusive. This lighting impact in the tearoom contributes enormously to the entire atmosphere as everything inside the space is bathed in a warm, calming glow. In addition to these shoji panels, good-quality paper has also been used as a basis for monochrome photographs for the scrolls hanging in the tearoom.

Paper uses: rollover windows. While specialist papers for making shoji screens are available in Japan, thin handmade papers can have a very similar effect. The frames can be constructed carefully or crafted from more organic forms.

• Wallpaper or unattractive wall coverings. Applied in a patch quilt form in the same manner as wallpaper, it has the impact of breaking down some of the walls ' visual solidity. The paper's natural colors and the differences in textures will bring a sense of warmth and comfort to a space. Framed hangings on the wall.

Other art bases. Many contemporary Japanese artists now use strong natural paints on a highly textured board, and the un-equality of the surface brings to the image a further complication.

Mats of the bed. A dense framed paper cut into mat sizes in lieu is an ideal way to add a more intimate feel to a setting table.

Light / lampshades filters. A small handmade sheet, which is fairly transparent, can be placed in a symmetrical or asymmetrical form around a wooden or metal frame to reduce the strength of a light source.

USING TEXTILES

While Japan is probably better known for the peerless silk work involved in making kimono, a cult of textile appreciation still exists which emphasizes tactile and visual complexity. The wabi-sabi component of fabrics is seen in coarse weaves and typical natural colors such as persimmon, tea, saffron, cabbage, and indigo are used. Such dyes are added to fabrics such as hemp, silk, and cotton, and the best way to achieve a wabi-sabi-style effect is to require a degree of randomness in the cycle so that there is an almost imperceptible stream of change in color throughout the fabric item.

The dyeing method often helps the hand of nature to work a spell into the cloth so there is a degree of imperfection that can be seen and savored as with all natural mediums.

There are several artists in Japan, including Kumozawa Fujiko, who make wall hangings and space dividers using textiles.

Kumozawa uses kaya as a foundation, an ancient mosquito net constructed of hand-woven hemp, and then applies a range of natural colours. These are then either framed downwards or weighted downwards.

A surprisingly good source of wabi-sabi textiles comes from less economically developed countries and the African conti-nent in particular. The use of natural dyes and the materials ' hand weaving ensures that the textiles have an added dimension of interest that is lacking in the consistency of most modern fabrics made from machines. The Zaire fabric shown on the previous page in the image, while somewhat more abstract than mere Japanese job, is a good example of the available material. The randomness and rawness match well with the fading organic colours. The African, who created it many decades ago, was probably closer to the wabi-sabi spirit than many tea practitioners of today, and the uninfluenced African spirit flows through every fiber of this fabric.

Textile uses: loose or mirrored hangings on the mirror. One might, for example, tie an enticing piece of cloth between two halves of bamboo and hang it with some hemp twine on a plain wall. Weights discreetly sown inside the bottom help to keep the material in place.

• Dividers of the room. The Japanese also split spaces that come down from the ceiling to about chest height, not with doors or full-length curtains but with cloth dividers. These have the effect of visually distinguishing non-door zones.

• Upholstery / curtains of furniture. Inner rooms look less cold and more welcoming when adding unique textures and natural dyes.

Floor tatami mats. Although not expressly wabi-sabi in their design, the traditional flooring for Japanese houses can bring an overall sense of naturalness to a room and tend to complement other accented pieces.

Clothes like that. It is very easy to bring a feeling of wabi-sabi to the closet, sticking to the ideals of muted colors, natural materials and simple lines. There are many designers in Japan who use wabi-sabi aesthetics to increase the appeal of their clothes.

Runners at the table and put mats.

USING ROCKS AND STONES

Though scarcely seen in Japanese interiors, rocks and stones played an essential role in the development of the Japanese artistic ideal. The forms carved by nature over millions of years make rocks and stones some of the oldest physical objects in our world, with some dating far beyond our capacity to conceive of the vastness of the passage of time. Melted deep within the earth, caught up in ice flows, pounded by rivers, eroded by rain, and ravished by extremes of heat and cold, rocks represent the most incredible resilience to the elements and yet even the hardest granite must eventually yield to the omni-potent forces at large. Perhaps in part it is the collision between these two immense powers and the research evolution has accomplished over endless centuries that renders rocks so irresistible in their appeal. The depths they have experienced are written on their surfaces as well as through their nuclei, and can practically be entrancing. Not to ignore such an obvious truth, the Japanese extensively integrated rocks into their garden designs and also created an art form named suiseki (water stones), which included literally placing unusual rocks located in the countryside on a carved wooden pedestal.

The use of flat stones or mined stones, however, was limited by the preference of wood as a building medium, and thus the use of processed stones, other than those carved for garden ornaments, was relatively limited. Throughout Tokyo today one can see the costly marbles and granites used for tower block façades, but there is still still minimal use of stone for interior decoration, and given its ability and the Japanese love of things shibui (literally "bitter" or "astringent") this seems a bit surprising. This may be explained in part by the limited usefulness of stone for interiors and the pre-form function criteria in Japan.

There are stone surfaces lying between the two extremes of polished marbled and naturally occurring rocks which are almost audible in their appeal for wabi-sabi. For illustration, the hand-run surface of the slate, with its numerous hints of orange green, brown, and iron lying on and between the intertwined layers, creates an image of its own right. Such stimulating properties can be used for making inlaid tabletops and other work surfaces in combination with other material, such as wood. A sanding of the untreated surface accompanied by a few coats of oil (it fits well with finishing wax) can leave a very desirable and sturdy coating.

Stone Uses: Table tops, functional surfaces. All of these fit well with granites, sandstone, slates and calcareous. Instead of using a highly polished board, the matte quality makes a riven or honed finish preferred.

Stonemasons often have slices of quarried stones with some very interesting shapes which still have their natural edges.

Integral furniture parts. To build a coffee table, a slab of slate or sandstone cut square may be placed into a wooden covering.

Stone manufacturers sometimes market slabs of this kind in precut sizes.

For tile and tiling. There are now plenty of various natural stones available in tile form which can give a natural feel to floors or tiled walls. The old flagstones found in English cottages are a perfect example of how an interior can complement the unevenly worn surface of the stones.

Contemplation stones (natural shaped stones / rocks). You can find these at the countryside. Carbon-iferous granite, igneous rocks, and also desert rocks are well matched to wabi-sabi aesthetics.

Features of the garden. In Japanese garden architecture, large rocks strategically placed either in gravel or foliage and asymmetrical stepping-stones have long been used. When planning a landscape in the UK Japanese. We found a large stone whose shape, texture and color we especially liked but it was hard to use in its original shape.

CLAY

Clay is at the heart of the wabi-sabi tradition and although a degree of sophistication is needed for molding and fire clays, there is still an abundance of interesting pieces that can be bought either new or second-hand. There is a deep-rooted dedication to pottery in Japan, as discussed in the section on pottery, and every conceivable effort has been made to bring its aesthetic potential to full success. A long-term effort is to pursue the research of Japanese pottery, and expertise in Japan may still be challenging to transfer into other countries. Nevertheless, there are a number of outlets outside of Japan for those interested in finding wabi-sabi bits of pottery, and searching them out can be an interesting affair indeed. As wabi-sabi is primarily interested in the artless and the humble, as with textiles, the first port of call is the countries where local crafts are often a substitute for modern technology.

If shopping for wabi-sabi pottery either overseas or at home the following are recommendations on what to look for: / Effective rather than decorative / Rough and raw feel / Little to no specified style / Soft, quiet colours, ideally with natural ash glaze / Complexity in color and texture / Naturality and ease of use We have now looked at the many different aspects of wabi-sabi nature, its ph.

It's as easy as hard to bring the feeling of wabi-sabi into a modern environment. The first and most important aspect of wabi-sabi is the attitude of mind towards art as well as life. This poses the huge challenge of reassessing our mindset toward our worlds, our fellow men and ourselves at the most fundamental level. Once our impermanence emphasizes the utter irrelevance of material gain and when we see our lives with a sense of humility and equanimity, then we are able to see the beauty which resides within the subtleties.

We begin to enjoy the artless and the ordinary as the esthetic rises and improves. This then extends to all aspects of life — relationships with others, our choice of employment, and the environments in which we choose to live. Slowly and without premeditation, we are gradually integrating the wabi-sabi designs into our living spaces until they become a natural extension of our own modest and unadorned affection.

Like the Taoism philosophy, where wabi-sabi finds its earliest roots, there is a need to approach wabi-sabi design with respect and gentleness. The wu-wei theory, or not pushing, is the basis for this gradual and normal acceptance of a world view of the wabi-sabi.

The potential of this personal journey is to bring greater harmony between the spiritual beings we are and the material world we live in. The living environments evolving from this understanding will help nurture our sensitivity to the world and foster a deeper shared appreciation of nature's artistry.

CHAPTER NINE: FINDING WABI-SABI IN EVERYTHING

- The esthetic and commitment to beauty in wabi-sabi involves embracing the cycle of natural aging–lines will arrive, creases will grow–and being able to recognize, appreciate and find happiness in the times that have passed.

There is a phenomenon in dental surgery that many Japanese women adhere to in order to achieve a perfect smile in their edition. It is called yaeba, and though it may be paradoxical, it is actually a crooked, out of line smile. The uniqueness of yaeba is that it reflects the vivacity of youth and the notion that an awkward, snaggletoothed grin due to its shortcomings is endearing and charming.

- In terms of bringing the esthetic of wabi-sabi into the house, it's worth thinking about this in this way: it's about the threadbare mattress, not the white leather sofa; the sticky stains on the wall; the wine stain on the new carpet. House is a living space and not a showroom. Minimalistic, clutter-free and natural; it has a place in our world, it relates to nature, but it is not flat, dull and without character or irony. Many Japanese houseware stores sell rustic and simply decorated items–where the central feature of unpainted wood is. Like a fine wine, over time, wood becomes better and more interesting as it starts telling stories and assumes its own character.

- I still consider things like new leather bags, a bit unsettling and awkward using brand-new objects. I need to get used to them, and they need to get used to me–they need to be part of my story, much as I need to be part of their life cycle.

A tube of hand sanitizer spilled at a music festival a few years ago all over a new designer wallet that I had saved up for and pur-chased as a birthday gift for myself. At the moment, I was sad, frustrated and angry, but it ended up reminding me of dancing in the boiling sun by my bed, staying up until 5 a.m. Listening to amazing artists and taking questionable decisions driven by misjudged plum brandy shots–both tales twisted into my life's cloth and literally represented in a dark stain on a battered old wallet.

Whenever someone asks me for the best time of the year to go to Japan, I never know how to reply–because each season has its unique benefits. The cherry blossoms are out in the morning, but the summer promises shaved ices, fireworks and the Bon Festival. The fall boasts spectacular leaves, while Japanese winter delights contain mild sake, snow and, if you're fortunate, red-crowned cranes. Time passage; rise, decay, and death; and understanding of the normal order of events is also a key part of wabi-sabi. For all of this, seeking contentment, compassion, and gratitude is at the root of what wabi-sabi is as a philosophy and mind-set; it is a way of life and understanding the world around us.

- Wabi-sabi is not about having the latest trend or acquiring new items; it is about rediscovering an old top at the back of your closet, or creating a delicious meal with the detritus in your fridge. It is not really about material possessions, or owning anything at all. "Frugal" doesn't seem to be the most appropriate word to use here and "thrifty" doesn't –because it's more about being canny and careful and doing. And by doing so, it's about achieving fulfillment, satisfaction and joy. Part of that has to do with the mentality of living in a place so full of earthquakes, tsunamis and other natural disasters. You are quite simply learning to let go.

- Perhaps the idea of ageing in Japan is not something that is shied away from as much as it is, maybe, in the West because of the massive (and increasing ever larger) elderly population. For the older generation, life in Japan is a little more welcoming. It continues even in a new setting, where trends are best catered for. For starters, there is a wide selection of smartphones designed specifically for the older consumer, which is constantly evolving.

Within the culture, the older generation holds a position of importance, and care for them is seen as a collective, social responsibility. Maybe that's why the idea of ageing is so clearly evident in Japan-because of the manner in which care for the elderly is historically treated. This is closely related to the idea of fureai-the shared relation or relationship that is established between generations or within community by different professions or vocations. Fureai is different from a more traditional relationship or friendship, which means "a close mutuality." It is used to describe the relationship an instructor in the kindergarten may have with their students, or a nurse might have with the patients in their supervision.

Items like fureai kippu (a "caring partnership ticket") will take hold and thrive within this type of environment. A fureai kippu introduced in the early 1990s became a form of social currency or credits reflecting an hour of community service which can be received or traded. This could be peer-to-peer, within the same generational group (where friends might help each other out with tasks such as, for example, popping up to the pharmacy), or between generations in return for errands, such as being driven somewhere or assisted with certain chores. So a younger person may receive those credits by transporting someone to the store, helping weeding the garden or physical or manual work that an elderly person is unable to do.

People with elderly families elsewhere can help in their own local community and then transfer their credits to their relatives so that, in turn, they can access similar services that their family might traditionally have provided if they had lived closer.

Basically, Fureai kippu is a tangible, tradable expression of altruism, in a bankable, exchangeable shape. Thanks to presumed personal connection, certain users of the fureai kippu scheme favor programs accessed through the society rather than those motivated through purely financial benefit. The bottom line is that age is not something to be scared of or shied away from - it's happening to us all. The lessons that can be learnt here are about empathy, kindness and supporting every step of their path to create a deeper, more compassionate, and welcoming community for everyone.

- As someone who earns a living from educating organisations on the positive and amazing things they can do with social media, I know firsthand how detrimental it can be.
There is constant pressure to post about how happy your life is, how much fun you have, or how great you look-all the while being surrounded by others doing the same thing. Yet remember to take everything with a grain of salt. No one likes to talk about their bad days or their aches and pains; be mindful that underneath the surface everything isn't always as rosy as it seems to be everywhere–and always compassionate. All of this ties in with a broader theme of

life's transience. Try to be present at all times, be real and be yourself. So, you're going to be happier.

- Many wabi or sabi objects can be considered shibui, too. This can be described as a subtle, understated, and refined, but humble or subdued kind of elegance that, while being at first glance seemingly plain, indicates a deeper complexity inside.

  The term behind the definition translates as being astringent or hard, but not with a negative connotation generally. Much can be shibui, in that they are simple, unassuming, uncomplicated. And it is the beauty and appeal which lie in their very functionality.

  "Austerity" is another term that could be used to express the meaning behind shibui, but it also contains an aspect of beauty and elegance. For example, shibui colors are subdued-especially grayer tones.

It's about enjoying the simpler things in life–without being overindulgent, or excessively extravagant, and finding the beauty and charm in the distressed, well-worn clothing item and how it can bring joy.

- Mono means "fact," and aware (pronounced ah-wah-reh) translates into empathy or gentle sorrow about the ephemeral, transitory nature of life. It can also imply openness to events and life's essence-something that is deliberately understood and embraced with a touch of sadness or wistfulness.

This is another way the Japanese language succeeds in capturing the nostalgic feelings we all experience. Recently, at a dinner party, I had a conversation with a friend who pointed out that at one point in your childhood, for the last time, your parent would pick you up or lift you onto their shoulders–and mono no consciousness encapsulates perfectly the feeling that thought evokes. It's a disappointment at that knowledge but also a sense of the inevitability of all of it. This arises from contemplation and knowledge of yourself, and from studying the wider world around you.

- I can always be heard to make frequent exclaims of "natsukashii" during the first few days of a tour back to Japan!"Natsukashii is a sentimental feeling of joy, or something that evokes some sort of emotion or memory. Mostly when I find a particular smell or consume something nice that I haven't had in a while, it occurs. Although mostly one of happiness, the feeling behind natsukashisii is always so slightly tinged with a wistful poignancy too. It's a happy and enjoyable feeling on balance though, and the kind you want to experience when you're down. You may get it when you see friends of old school or when you think about old habits or things that you may have been phasing out of your existence. For starters, flicking through old albums or listening to music from a certain point in your life is a great way to bring relaxation and take stock.

- I assume that wabi-sabi speaks to so many outside of Japan as a philosophy because it compares with other values of success–the relentless pursuit of beauty, the stagnant or the flawlessness. Such values are completely unrealistic and unattainable in many respects, and almost ungraceful. It seems more forgiving to find comfort and beauty in the passage of the moment, and to be relaxed in accepting what we cannot change. It makes it possible to find peace and contentment, and encourages you to be more observant and childlike to yourself.

Wabi-sabi brings you back to the core of what it means to be human and to your connection with natural processes and the path you are on - how easily life sneaks up on you and how necessary it is to count your blessings.

CHAPTER TEN: WABI-SABI IN KINTSUGI

Kintsugi is the craft of restoring golden-lacquered cracked pottery. Shattered bits are put back together and decorated with gold becoming even more exquisite than they were initially. An item becomes more treasured than ever, rather than being rejected or hated for its defects, as its disfigurement or weakness becomes its power through the practice of kintsugi, contributing to its charm.

Kintsugi is often found in the tea ceremony (or sado) cups, where pieces with an interesting imperfection or defect are highly prized for their beauty and aesthetic quality.

The definition of kintsugi is a convincing term and not just refers to artifacts. It's a significant one, and even inspiring one to talk about, particularly at those hard times in your life. It may even apply to something as trivial as a feature or "flaw" that you perceive within yourself. I have always had a freckled nose, for starters. I've spent countless hours and a lot of money covering up and covering up the blemishes that show on my skin when I've been out in the sun for too long.

Growing up, there was always a single freckle I despised–on my lip, just off center, just to the top. In my dismay, I would hide it fully with concealer in an attempt to make it disappear, which it never completely did.

Then, during my first year at college-an incredibly awkward time of life when you're trying to make friends and find your feet in a new city and surroundings-someone who would later become one of my closest friends mentioned how much she liked this hated freckle. It was just a passing remark, made as we prepared for a night out, but since then, that mark on my chin has always made me think of her, that time in my life, and how much fun we have together. This turned the freckle into one of my favorite features from a blemish.

I appreciate the Kintsugi theory because the challenges that we encounter really form who we are as individuals. Much as you need the sour to experience the good, the challenges we face — loss, deceit, heartbreak, deception — are part of our history, our personalities, and our tales. And instead of hiding the scars they are leaving, kintsugi encourages us to celebrate them, and the ways they serve to define us. Nothing is ever really broken, no matter how painful that may sound at the time.

It also helps us to be more aware and respectful of customers on a more practical level. Rather than indulging in fast fashion, we can look after our belongings, concentrating on the repair process rather than simply discarding and swapping with something different. It's better for the environment, it's safer for our bank accounts and it also takes on waste.

Instead, kintsugi is also a powerful metaphor for how we approach our perceived strengths and weaknesses. There is a Japanese phrase that expresses this so well–chousho wa tansho, which loosely translates into "Our strengths are our weaknesses." While we least anticipate it, over-reliance on or over-confidence in our supposed strengths will trap us.

It's an important lesson not to take for granted the qualities that we find to be assets–they all require work, commitment and a lot of nurturing, whether it's a talent, a friendship, or our (mental and physical) wellbeing.

It is finding, and celebrating, joy and beauty in imperfection which makes kintsugi so powerful.

Kintsugi is so amazing because it really highlights a pivotal moment in an object's existence–the stage where it breaks under strain. But it also shows that the object can still retain its magnificence–that the moment it cracks in a longer, more important journey is merely a small step.

Kintsugi can be viewed as a symbol for enduring defeat or deception, showing not the loss itself but how it influenced the entity or person in question. This plays an important role in the tea ceremony and shows much about the psychology and cultural values in that phase–kintsugi tea cups and other so-called faults and imperfections are valued above those that are meant to be flawless. The flaws, chips, repairs, and cracks also reveal much more about the owner's relationship with the objects: how well they are taken care of, how loved, how dependent they are, and the integral part they play in somebody's practice.

Much of all this is in the beholder's head, but it can also be similar to somebody's friendship with their teddy bear from childhood. It will never be as beautiful to another person, who does not have that intense relationship with him–yet it will be obvious to see, from the patchwork, the repairs, and the worn materials, that the object is loved, and that it has played a significant role in the life of its owner.

CONCLUSION: HUMILITY, CONTENTMENT AND MODESTY IN THE JAPANESE CULTURE

Humility or modesty is one of the most important aspects of Japanese proper conduct. In Japanese society, people are expected to be humble regardless of their social position; that is, they have to learn how to properly modulate the specific show of ability, intelligence, or money. Self-assertiveness is more or less discouraged while empathy is promoted for others. This mentality is reflected in a popular Japanese saying, "The nail that sticks up gets hammered down" (Deru kui wa utareru), which suggests that those who display their talents are at risk of being smashed by others quite publicly. On the other side, there are other old sayingings that extol the virtues of modesty, such as "The ears of a rice plant grow ripe and hang small" (Bosatsu miga ireba utsumuku), which implies that, rather than being arrogant and haughty, it is important to be humble and respectful, even when one is more advanced, more accomplished and more polished than others.

The meaning of these sayings is successful in maintaining the Japanese people's collective culture, and their mindset should continue in society as long as there are noble and respectful modes of expression (keigo) in Japanese. As far as intercultural communication is concerned, the value of humility in Japanese culture also causes confusion and mixed messages because it results in the Japanese engaging with people from other nations creating too much self-deprecation or self-effacement.

In interpersonal relationships Japanese culture is organized into fine lines of vertical hierarchy leading to degrees of control and space. For example, while employees in the company may be similar in terms of ability, they are always ranked by age, year of entry into the organization and length of continuous service. A senior or an elder is named a sempai; a kōhai is one who is younger or junior.

The sempai-kōhai dichotomy is present in nearly every industrial, educational, and governmental institution in Japan.

Children are usually not fully aware of those vertical interactions before children graduate from elementary school. However, they're expected to conform to this rigid system as soon as they enter junior high school. This is particularly true for extracurricular activities that are performed in Japan with little adult supervision and that take place within a rigid hierarchical structure. Sempai are allowed to' place on air' with kōhai, but if kōhai pass sempai without courteously greeting them, they are considered insolent (namaikina yatsu) and given the cold shoulder, or sometimes much worse. In this vertical structure students are trained through Japanese group dynamics and know how to get along with each other.

Relationships between Sempai and Kōhai are prevalent not only in Japanese schools or universities but also in companies and even groups of ikebana (flower arrangement). Once people enter society, there are not only many sempai, but also many clients and business connections, all of which need to be carefully treated. That is the essence of Japanese humility. Even though there seems to be a growing sense of egalitarianism today, people are still aware of those hierarchies. Indeed, even the arrangements for seating and the order of speeches at weddings and banquets are done strictly according to rank. In Japan, well-educated people are supposed to know their position; to abide by the tacit rules of society, which first designate "superiors;" and to naturally show their modesty. To this end there are honorable and humble forms of the language.

In the Japanese society and to anyone in the world who is willing to appreciate their flaws and brokenness, and yet embrace it and wear it with pride, then WABI-SABI provides the ultimate opportunity for you. Thanks for reading!!!